Sustainovation

Building *sustainable innovation* in government,
one wildly creative idea at a time.

CONTENTS

FOREWARD

This book has been years in the making, and I might even argue my whole life. I'm grateful to have the chance to share what I've learned in my time as a government innovator and hopefully spread concepts that make innovation in government stick.

My professional experiences have been enriched through the partnership and wisdom of so many great people along the way, so I want to thank just a few of them including Alicia Archibald, Allen Peterson, Allison Plute, Brandi Rank, Carrie McCausland, Cheryl Rea, Curt DeCapite, Frank Kinder, Heather McDermott, Jay Anderson, Jeff Bowman, Jeff Newsome, John Olson, Julia Ferguson, Linda Kogan, Manny Navarro, Mary Barber, Meghan Riesterer, Mike Anderson, Nancy Johnson, Penny Culbreth-Graft, Rafael Natividad, Tim Hodur, and Tom Monarco. Each of you has taught me something about myself, my abilities and what it means to rely on an amazing team. You have been my Team Us (among so many more)—so thank you.

I also want to thank a few of my very close friends who have been such a great support through the years including Brian Potts, Brian Conly, Brian Rockey, Felicity Beckman, Kelly Wabbington, Kyle Hart, Matt Craig, Paul McLaughlin, and Roy Beckman. You are amazing and I'm so glad to call you my friends. And to my dear friend Kevin Davis who is no longer with us, I will never forget your gregariousness and loyalty. I've learned more from each of you than I could have possibly imagined.

In addition, my deepest appreciation to Adrian Newman of Newman Designs for his amazing work in the graphic design and layout of this book and his sick disc golf skills —you really know how to make an idea come to life! And to Sue Fody of Got It! for her engaging illustrations.

And most importantly, I want to thank my family: my mom DeAnn who showed me what the heart of an artist means and how to see fearlessly, my mom Vicky who showed me that our best self is about supporting others and giving selflessly, and my dad, Dan, who showed me the meaning of leadership, made sure my thirst for knowledge was insatiable and my standard of work high. I want to say thank you to my sister Casey for being my first best friend and my most honest and fierce fan, my sister Milea for her insane talent and excellence, and my sister Brittany for being the most electric and dynamic of us all! And last but not least, I want to honor the memory of my younger brother Zack for his rogue's spirit and zest for life. Your time on this planet ended too soon, and we will see each other on the other side soon enough. You better practice your wrestling.

But most especially I want to thank my supportive and amazing wife LeeAnn, my daughter Alyssia, her mother Heather, and my son Kai.

Kai, I can't wait to watch you grow up and teach you about this life, and learn more about who you are. You're already a part of my heart and I can't wait to get to know you more! Alyssia, I couldn't be prouder of the young lady you've already become, and all you've taught me about this world. You're a gifted storyteller, a soft heart, a bright light and I hope I can teach you as much as you've taught me. I hope neither of you ever lose your sense of curiosity and wonder.

Heather, thank you for being an amazing mother to our daughter, and one of the kindest souls I know.

And most of all to my talented, creative and beautiful wife LeeAnn. THANK YOU for encouraging me, supporting me and inspiring me. You're my very favorite human. That's it. Just my favorite person on this spinning, floating rock we call Earth. Thanks for being my muse, standing by me every step of the way, and pushing me to be my best. This book is as much a testament to your influence, as it is my work.

To all of you and so many more who have influenced and supported me, remember to live the live you love, and love the life you live. Now let the wild rumpus start!

SUSTAINOVATION

This book is a how-to guide on creating sustainable innovation, or *Sustainovation*. For you. For your organization. For your community. Like an innovation superpower, if you will. Head's up: This is not a safe, scrubbed, academic document about the theory of innovation, but a practitioner's guide to innovation success—in government.

You see, I am a civic innovator. For those who don't know what a civic innovator is, it is a champion of the possible inside government. Someone whose job it is to fight back against "because that's the way we've always done it." In 2008, there were fewer than 50 of us in a room, and today there are thousands of people in a career related to the innovation field in government—people whose job it is to reimagine the future of our communities and our country.

And yes, I proudly help create innovation for *government*. But before you laugh too much, can you imagine anything more necessary, and more critical than innovation in government? We face massive challenges as community leaders, and the challenges we face today will not be solved by the same thinking that created them. Our quality of life, our economy, and our very societies hang in the balance of our ability to implement creative, novel solutions to problems that impact us all. So, we must innovate. But how?

After more than a decade of doing this, I am more excited than ever about the power great innovation can have on government and the lives of citizens as well as its effects on our society. It also surprises me how rare it is to see targeted innovation efforts in government organizations, despite the overwhelming need. We are talking about the single largest employer in the world, the government, with no R&D department? Come on! We talk about innovation in communities across the world, but how are we training our employees and ourselves? For most organizations, it's as if we hope the innovation fairy just "happens" to dust our employees with magical innovation dust. And just like any other field, we must train and practice innovating to be good at it. *Sustainovation* is not a miracle; it's an intentional effort.

The cool part is that if we practice and train on innovation, we will be generating our own creative ideas on how to service our communities. I encourage communities I train and work with to look "inside the box," because employees are part of our communities as well. Not only that, but as government employees, we also understand how government works, where it doesn't, and where it needs to work better. We can use that knowledge to defend existing practices and "the way we've always done things," or use our knowledge to attack opportunities to improve the lives of our citizens with a vengeance. As both a resident and someone empowered to make change, we become the critical piece of the innovation equation for government. We are the ones with the ability to reinvent or influence policy, eliminate red tape, build critical programs, reduce taxpayer burdens, provide outstanding service, save lives, and so much more. And that is a powerful responsibility. By building *Sustainovation* in our communities, we can train ourselves and our employees to be change agents and begin to move a culture that doesn't traditionally value innovation, but desperately needs to. I've seen it happen in organizations throughout my career, and I believe it can happen in any organization with the right training and a handful of highly-motivated individuals.

That's why I find myself writing this. It's not that I believe I have all the answers to innovation in government—far from it—but I do believe that the lessons I share here can help you hit the fast-forward button by unlocking the creativity of your employees. That is my goal: to share what I know so we can transform our organizations and achieve a pattern of sustained innovation: *Sustainovation*.

Becoming a gifted practitioner of *Sustainovation* requires a commitment to embracing the unusual, bizarre, silly, and downright puzzling. It requires growing an extra layer of skin at times, finding the right team, and selling it. It requires urgency and inspiration, and above all, creativity. It requires practice, and the tips, tricks and lessons contained in this book will help anyone start down a path of *Sustainovation* that can create millions of dollars in savings and transform the lives of our communities.

How to Use This Book

One of the challenges I came across when writing this book is that innovation is not linear, but people seem to expect a linear narrative arc in a book, so that makes writing about it a challenge. For me, *Sustainovation* and building innovation is akin to baking. We need some basic, key ingredients to get going on most recipes: salt, sugar, flour, water, eggs, oil, butter, etc. We may not need all of them for every dish, but we will undoubtedly need at least one or more of these ingredients, and if we're missing the wrong one, the dish doesn't work. Consider these the major ingredients of this book—the chapters.

Just like baking a recipe, there can be many variations that work, but the key ingredients remain the same. Some innovation "ingredients" require more study, practice, and use than others. We also need different spices to give our innovation dish flavor and flair. While there were dozens more techniques I could have included in this book, and ultimately eliminated, I tried to limit it to ten key themes in each major chapter section to make this book easier to follow and use. We must learn to grab the right innovation ingredients as we need them, and that takes practice.

So as you read this, please remember to think of what we are discussing as ingredients in our innovation kitchen. Each innovation recipe requires different skills, and we won't need every technique every time. We won't need them in equal measure, but we should have them on hand for when we do. Each innovation effort is different and requires us to evaluate which techniques are most effective to get the best results, but consider this book your spice rack for innovation.

Oh, and by the way, you each have your own ingredients and spice racks already! Some of these ideas you've heard before or used yourself; some you haven't. Some will resonate more than others, and that's okay. Different strokes for different folks. The tips, tricks, thoughts, and observations you find here are hard-won over years of building innovation programs and *actually doing* innovation in government. My hope is that these will help you find your *Sustainovation* chef's hat.

PHILOSOPHY, RIVERS AND PARADOXES

Why is innovation hard?

Innovation is hard for many of us for several reasons. In many cases, we are not trained to employ the creative side of our brains. In fact, it is actively trained out of many of us during our schooling. In other cases, we do not have an environment that supports innovation. In some cases, we are unable to convince others we need to take the risk with us. And sometimes, we do not have the necessary framework. There are many more reasons that innovation is a challenge for us, but there are also many things we can do to create an environment more suited to being successful.

The truth is, innovation is not a "one size fits all" endeavor. It is adaptable and fluid, requiring different skills for different situations. It is an art *and* a science, and it requires us to use abilities most of us rarely cultivate once we get in school, let alone once we get "in the business world." Therefore, innovation is hard.

Philosophy vs Process

Innovation is part philosophy and part process. Most books try to reduce it to one or the other, and the fact is, innovation is not exclusively one or the other. Great, sustained innovation requires us to understand the philosophy that leads to original thought and the process of how to do it, as well as the philosophy of how to take action, and the steps to get an idea off the ground and sell it.

Muddying the waters further, government is particularly bad at co-opting the word "innovation" to mean many other things. Innovation and efficiency and technology and smart cities are not synonyms and are not interchangeable—nor are they mutually exclusive. Just different. So when we conflate these terms, we do a disservice to what they can help us do: improve the lives of our citizens.

Innovation is not exclusively technology—it is the creative application of technology to solve real problems. It is not just "smart cities," but it is the boundary-pushing design elements that change the future of our community fabric. It's not open data, but it is using that data to solve problems and make government accessible in ways never before possible. It is also a first-of-its-kind pavement resurfacing program, a first-time Styrofoam collection event, an experimental xeriscaping ordinance, and an arts program in the lobby of a building. It is the creative application of efficiency programs, but it is not the same as efficiency.

To help illustrate the point, think about the automobile being invented by Karl Benz before the turn of the 20th century. At the time, there was nothing efficient about the idea of a car when you think about the infrastructure (roads, bridges), fuel (refineries, shipping, processing), manufacturing, capital, etc., that are needed—especially in the 1880s; but it certainly was innovative! If the focus had been on efficiency, not innovation, Karl Benz would have invented a more effective horse and buggy, and we would not have taken a quantum leap forward as a society. Sometimes efficiency and innovation are the same thing, but many times they are not.

On the other hand, efficiency is a great tool to find opportunities for creativity to be implemented, so these principles are related. We should recognize that just because a process is efficient for our residents, it doesn't mean that it is *creatively* addressing the residents' needs. In addition, there is a limit to efficiency or technology, whereas creativity knows no bounds. We can use efficiency to identify where a process needs improvement, but this does not increase our capacity to be creative in how we solve that problem. Efficiency doesn't create solutions to problems that don't yet exist, but creativity does. Both are needed in healthy measure to move the organizational needle and build better government, but let's acknowledge that they are not synonymous.

Similarly, technology can be innovative, but it is not exclusively innovation. Innovation is about creating new, impactful ways of thinking to replace old ways of thinking, not necessarily improving the systems that currently exist to be more digitized. The need for innovation shifts constantly. Technology is often a valuable tool to use, and many times provides a great launching point, but it is not the same thing as innovation.

The truth is, most of us haven't practiced, flexed, stressed, and stretched our *Sustainovation* muscles as often as we should, and so they are languishing—that is if we were ever trained to use them at all.

The River Of Our Experience

Why is innovation so hard for most of us? It's a worthy question, given the amount of time we talk about it and our organizations' claim to value it. The reason is our brains become more engrained over time to respond to the same things in the same way. The more we age, the more our experience shapes how we think.

Think of it like rain drops hitting a hillside. As the rain hits in the same spot, it rolls down the hillside in the same way over and over, carving a deeper and deeper path for the water. After time, this path is so deep, it has carved a river that flows very naturally in one direction: The *River of our Experience*. As we get older, this gets deeper.

As you can imagine, the more we have experiences of the same kind, the more we file the "right" path to deal with them. This means the older we get, the harder it is to shake up how we think, because our experience fights against our creativity. This is useful for most of life, as life would be insanely difficult if we had to relearn to tie our shoes or drive a car every single day. Instead, we use our *Rivers* to guide our day-to-day automation. So it is no wonder we don't actively practice fighting against our *River*. For the most part, it is incredibly useful—until it comes to innovation. Now we must learn something new. We must learn to shape a new path and reshape the *River*, and then be able to reshape it again in the future to handle a new flow of ideas. We must traumatize the hillside of our mind in some way to change the flow of our *River*. A flood of rain or a mudslide. Heavy equipment. This is how we shift our mental patterns and something I actively practice.

We will examine more about reshaping our *River* for innovation a little later. For now, just understand how we are fighting against our natural instincts in order to become better innovators, so it's no wonder innovation is hard for many of us, and that it is even harder for us to sustain.

> ### ✐ EXERCISE:
> Take out a sheet of paper and sign your name as many times as you can in one minute. How many times? Now do the same thing and sign your name—with your *opposite* hand. How many times with that hand? Why is this so difficult?
>
> There is nothing more fundamental than signing our own names. We have been doing it our whole lives. It is typically one of the first things we learn. It becomes engrained in our brains at a certain point, and our signatures become "fixed" in our minds as the "right way" to sign. But the fact is, it is difficult for most of us to sign our names with the opposite hand because we are not able to shake the *River of our Experience*.

The Innovation Paradox

Obviously, the *River of our Experience* shapes much of the challenge of innovation, but there is another force at play too. It's what I call the innovation paradox: As we get older, it typically becomes harder for us to be creative because we are unable to shake off the *River of our Experience*, and the creativity is trained out of us by our school and work environments. When we are younger, it is hard to innovate because we typically lack the ability to *implement* our ideas.

Yet, there are numerous examples of young entrepreneurs and innovators creating great ideas and disruptive products when they have the means and resources to implement them, but very few people are naturally prepared by their upbringing to be great innovators. Luckily, it is not hard to learn to flex these atrophied muscles with a little practice.

You see, the innovation paradox is that innovation occurs when uncommon ability to be creative crosses with uncommon ability to implement an idea. *In essence, to sustain innovation—to build Sustainovation—we must understand that innovation is creativity implemented and become more effective at both creativity and implementation.* We must be part artist and part scientist. We must cultivate both skill sets in parallel. And that is not how most of us are trained to behave or think as we grow up. Hence, we prize innovation because it is so rare, but it is so rare because we don't train people how to do it. The innovation paradox.

Consider this: It is not hard for children to dream up the concept of a flying car. But it is nearly impossible for kids to think of how they might "build" a flying car. You just "build it." Unfortunately, there is a practical reality involved with implementing this kind of innovation: What are the mechanics of such a vehicle? How do you set up a factory for production? Who would fund it? How much would you charge? Is there a market? But as an adult, we are limited by our "practical" mind that eliminates the flying car as a valuable and viable contribution to society as much as we might "wish" it to be so. We take it for granted that if it made sense, a company like Ford or Volkswagen would have built it already. Inherently, we no longer think about the concept of making a flying car because we are limited by the "rules" of society that chase this idea from our mind as being impractical and therefore not worthy of further development or thought. The electric vehicle was a forgotten farce until Elon Musk made it not only possible, but affordable, cool, and powerful. At one point, the same was true of the light bulb, the automobile, the computer, and just about every other invention that we now take for granted. The idea was considered silly or impractical until the right person came along to unlock its potential.

So, it is those points in time, where uncommon creativity crosses with an uncommon ability to implement, that we find the nexus of great *sustained* innovation. Without these "shifts" in our creativity, or without our ability to implement, we are limiting our ability to innovate. For those who can make the shift, like Elon Musk, innovation is not only practical or plausible, it is a constant reality. He had to demonstrate exceptional creativity as well as exceptional implementation skills to bring the Tesla to market. And now, it is the fastest production car in the world and has the least impact on the environment of any vehicle out there. There is no reason we all can't unleash these kinds of tools in ourselves. But he trained. He tinkered. He tried. He convinced. He survived ridicule and opposition. And his organization reflects that: uncommonly strong creativity coupled with uncommonly strong implementation. And in the end, his company has already succeeded in creating amazing innovations, and will create many more. He employs the principles of *Sustainovation* throughout his company, and he is happy to go where no one has gone before (cue the *Star Trek* theme song music). Which brings me to an important question.

Map Maker Or A Map Follower?

In my experience, there are two types of innovators: those who make the maps, and those who follow them. It is important for us to understand what kind of innovator we are on a given project as well as what kind we want to be. *Map Makers* are people who create disruption in markets or thinking. *Map Followers* are the people who make the disruptions or the thinking better. We remember both, and both are incredibly valuable throughout human history.

Map Makers

To be a disruptive innovator, it is necessary to become a *Map Maker*. This means becoming comfortable with the unknown. This means sailing off the edge of the world or tromping boldly through the wilderness. This requires a courage that a *Map Follower* doesn't always use. We are all familiar with stories about the famous explorers—for good or bad—such as Lewis and Clark, Christopher Columbus, Edmund Hilary, Jacques Cousteau, and Neil Armstrong. Their courage to challenge the unknown is legendary.

Being first does not always lead to the greatest success, but it leads to disruption that can cause a shift in how the world looks at itself. People remember Lewis and Clark and the Wright Brothers but don't remember those that came after. Those that came before and were unsuccessful are also not household names.

Being a *Map Maker* is about charting a new course and being resilient. It's about having a willingness to fail and understanding that the greatest failure is not trying at all. The mindset of a *Map Maker* is to build a path for others to follow.

> *"You cannot discover new oceans unless you have the courage*
> *to lose sight of the shore." - André Gide*

Map Followers

But being first is not the only path to innovation—being better is too! *Map Followers* are creatively iterating and improving upon a blazed path and sometimes are even more successful than their predecessors at making an innovation real. *Map Followers* are great at iterating from someone else's idea and making innovations that are more functional, more comfortable, more usable, and more effective.

We remember Thomas Edison for inventing the lightbulb, but what he really did was improve it from existing concepts and make it commercially available—and it took him over 1,000 attempts to get it right. The idea of electric lighting was not new. Several people had worked on and developed forms of electric lighting. But up to that time, nothing had been developed that was remotely practical for the home. Edison's achievement was inventing not just an incandescent electric light but also an electric lighting system that contained all the elements necessary to make the incandescent light practical, safe, and economical. He accomplished this when he could come up with an incandescent lamp with a filament of carbonized sewing thread that burned for thirteen and a half hours.

There are a couple of other interesting things about the invention of the light bulb. While most of the attention has been given to the discovery of the ideal filament that made it work, the invention of seven other system elements were just as critical to the practical application of electric lights as an alternative to the gas lights that were prevalent in that day.[i]

THESE ELEMENTS INCLUDE:
- The parallel circuit
- A durable light bulb
- An improved dynamo
- The underground conductor network
- The devices for maintaining constant voltage
- Safety fuses and insulating materials
- Light sockets with on-off switches

And before Edison could make his invention work, every one of these elements had to be tested through careful trial and error and developed further into practical, reproducible components.

Alexander Fleming was the person who is credited with discovering penicillin, but he was unable to produce it commercially, in large part because of his notoriously poor communication skills. He could not implement and sell his innovation. But penicillin for use as a medicine is attributed to *Map Followers* Australian Nobel laureate Howard Walter Florey, together with the German Nobel laureate Ernst Chain and the English biochemist Norman Heatley. Without the medicine being commercially

i https://www.thoughtco.com/thomas-edisons-inventions-4057898

available, it could not be used for its highest and best purpose—helping people heal and saving countless lives.

Apple was not the first in the smart phone market, but Apple has been the best in the smart phone market. Remember the Simon? Well it was the first smart phone put out by IBM 13 years before the first iPhone. Don't remember it? *Exactly.* The iPhone was an example of doing it better

These are good examples of the how *Map Followers*, while differing from *Map Makers*, can achieve wild success with innovation. Both types of innovators are incredibly important to our innovation history and innovation economy. So, in the game of innovation, being first matters. But so does being better.

What is important is to determine the type of innovation needed for the circumstance. Is it something disruptive or is it something that improves on an existing concept? That will help you determine what the resistance is likely to look like. If it is disruptive change, it will require a strong intestinal fortitude to proceed, but if its iterative, it may be a matter of finesse and readiness to sell your idea to others. And yes, we will discuss techniques that I've personally used to build your armor and to build your momentum for those *Map Maker* moments, as well as how to get better at selling and implementing our ideas when we're working as *Map Followers*. Both have tremendous value, but the skills needed may be different.

Now that we understand our innovation challenges and the styles we can use, let's look at how to build *Sustainovation*.

Innovation Is Creativity Implemented

There are many definitions of innovation, and as I've gone through the years, I've find most of them to be inadequate, so for me, the most effective definition to understand the two key elements of any innovation is *creativity implemented*. To innovate effectively, we must be able to do both. We must shake off the innovation paradox and traumatize The *River of our Experience* to do this. The varying degrees to which people can be creative or implement an idea effectively determines the level at which they can succeed with *Sustainovation*.

To be successful in sustaining innovation, we need to explore the two halves of this innovation equation and dive into them. As I thought about the most successful innovations I've undertaken, there were common themes that emerged—top half of the following drawing being the keys to creativity, and the bottom half being the keys to implementation. The core of the image, or the nucleus, represents how we build *Sustainovation* by insulating it and institutionalizing it. The top half of the image includes the creativity drivers including "Why?", "Creativity and Perspective", "Growing Ideas" and "Pilot. Pilot. Pilot." Pilot projects represent the tipping point in innovation where we put creativity into practice. The bottom half of the image shows the keys to successful implementation. Implementation begins with building "*Team*

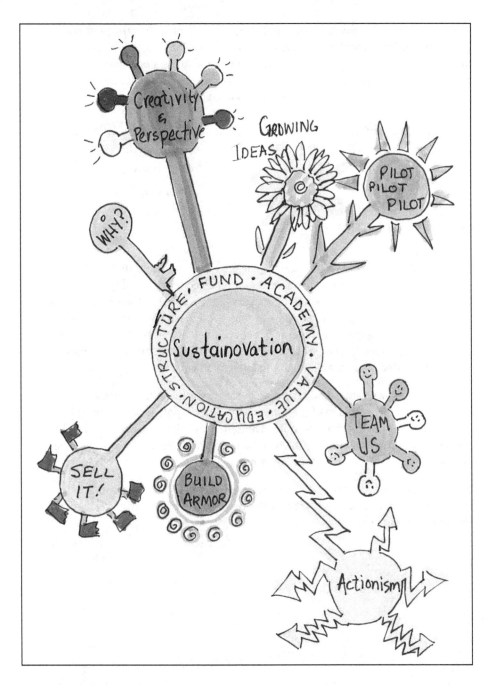

Us," understanding "Actionisms," learning how to "Build Armor," and then "Sell It."
Once we understand how to use these ingredients in our innovation kitchen and
get a little practice, we can bake *Sustainovation* into our organizations by creating
mechanisms to protect and institutionalize innovation using the FAVES.

The remainder of the book is dedicated to better understanding the elements of creativity and implementation—and all the principles that help you become better at both. There are exercises, anecdotes, and key questions along the way in the book that will help you understand and explore principles, and the more you use the techniques you find here, the better you will become.

CREATIVITY	IMPLEMENTATION
Why?	Team US
Creativity & Perspective	Actionisms
Growing Ideas	Build Your Armor
Pilot. Pilot. Pilot.	Sell It

For innovation to be wildly successful, it must be creative. Ideas that are first of their kind. Ideas that are wild or edgy. Ideas that are better. Ideas that improve. Ideas that disrupt. But how do you think of concepts that are first of their kind, or how do you come up with a better way of doing things? You must first learn to unlock your creativity. There are many techniques, as you will see, and learning and building skills around your creative talents, which we *all* have to a varying degree, can improve our ability to be effective in the first half the innovation equation.

But great ideas are just that: ideas. To be innovative, they must be *implemented*. Just because I have the idea of the time machine or perpetual motion machine doesn't mean I'm innovative. Now, if I invented one of those things, that would be unbelievable, and that's why it would be innovative. We must make the idea a reality. We must become adept at implementing as well.

It is equal parts art and science. Philosophy and process. Creativity and implementation. And we must train both sides of our brains to adopt and adapt to become adept at innovating.

START WITH "WHY?"

To begin, let's correct the spelling of the word: I believe that *"Why?"* is actually the correct spelling of the word because of how many people treat "why" as a four-letter word, which to a certain extent, it is. *W-H-Y-?* If you have ever asked someone *Why?* unexpectedly, you've probably had them stare back at you like you've been cursing at them. People sometimes react to *Why?* as if it offends them in the same way as profanity. *Why?* is viewed as a direct assault on a belief, and not unlike a curse word is an assault on our personal judgment. Some people have no problem at all with it, and some are deeply offended. But it is the most important question we can ask to understand the real nature of a problem, so we need to get good at asking.

The power of asking *Why?* as a tool for problem solving is well documented for finding the root cause, lean process improvement, Simon Sinek's TED talk, books, webinars, countless philosophical works, and far more, so I will spare you my compelling case and rehashing why using *Why?* is valuable. Just know that it is, and get more comfortable with using it. Practice asking it with empathy and understanding, and minimize any confrontational tone.

It is critical that we understand the *Why?* of what we are doing and what we are after. There are many ways and reasons we need to do this, but the *Why?* is a critical part of problem solving and ideation as well as the most important thing we can understand when speaking with others. It allows us to use passion and persuasion to entice others to our innovation cause and can become critical in our storytelling later.

How To Use "Why?"

The basic premise of being able to ask *Why?* effectively is to ask "why" five times—or until you run out of answers. When that happens, you've reached the core of the problem. Then begin solving for that. If you are doing this with a group, prepare everyone that you'd like to ask some questions to help understand the root cause of the challenge. This will minimize suspicion of your motives, help the group understand where you are going, and hopefully serve as a PG-13 warning that *Why?* is ahead.

My favorite anecdote to underscore this technique involves a story regarding the Lincoln Memorial. You see, there was a problem a few years ago where the stone was beginning to deteriorate.[ii] The issue began getting more and more attention from patrons, and the executives finally asked staff, "Why is the stone deteriorating?"

The maintenance crew responded, "Because of the high-power sprayers we use to wash the memorial every two weeks." Obviously not washing the memorial was not an effective option, so the executives asked, "Why are we doing high-powered washings every two weeks?"

The maintenance crew said, "Because of the bird droppings." So, the executives figured getting rid of the birds was the solution and had the crew install netting, which was unsightly and ineffective.

So, the maintenance crew was called again, and the executives asked, "Why are there so many birds?" They pointed out what seemed obvious to them: "The reason the birds come is to feed on the spiders," they said. "Spiders? Why are there so many spiders?" asked the executives. "Because there are billions of insects," said the crew.

As a result, the executives ordered the crews to use insecticides, which again proved ineffective and drew complaints, so the executives asked, "Why are there so many insects?" The crew responded that the insects were attracted by the high-powered spotlights shining on the memorial, particularly at dusk and dawn. The reason they shined the lights were for the tourists, so shutting them off completely did not make sense, but by adjusting the timing on the lights to come on 30 minutes after sunset and turn off 30 minutes before the sunrise, the bug problem virtually disappeared, and they saved money on energy costs.

Less light at dusk and dawn meant fewer bugs. Fewer bugs meant fewer spiders. Fewer spiders meant fewer birds. Fewer birds meant fewer droppings. Fewer droppings meant less washings. Less washings meant less deterioration of the stone on the outside of the memorial. It was the *Why?* that helped them get there.

Solve The Right Problem

And if we listen to the answer of *Why?* carefully, we can find the right problem or problems to solve. Whenever possible, strive to find the core of the issue before only treating the symptoms. And yes, in government, sometimes treating the symptoms is all we can do because of political realities, but we should always strive to solve for the root cause first.

For over a decade, a rare cancer has been sweeping through the Tasmanian Devil population, decimating it. The cancer is transferrable and creates large tumors along the face and jaw that eventually kill the infected devil. As the cancer spreads,

---

ii https://wallbuilder.wordpress.com/2013/05/29/the-lincoln-memorial-and-the-5-whys/

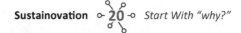

researchers realized there was a population of northern Tasmanian devils that appeared to be immune, or at least less susceptible, to the ravages of the disease, so they began testing these populations for differences that might make them resistant in ways the "southern" Tasmanian devils were not. Unfortunately, after two years of research, they discovered that this population was just as susceptible, but the cancer that was infecting them had morphed into a less infectious variety in the north. Fundamentally, the disease had changed, not the resistance of the animal. This also meant that the researchers are now turning their attention to "morphing" the cancer into its less dangerous counterpart. As you can see, solving the wrong problem can lead to ineffective outcomes, so solving the right problem is important to find working solutions. And finding the right problem can depend on whether there is already an existing process or product in place, or whether this is unfamiliar territory. This will help us determine whether we need to have our *Map Maker* or *Map Follower* hat on as we solve the right problem.

Parting Thoughts...

There are many reasons for learning how to use "Why?" better as it helps us understand the root cause of a problem, identifies our urgent and compelling reason to act, and sets the stage for developing innovative ideas that solve meaningful problems, but beware—not many people will like the question *Why?* But even though people may not like the question, get good at asking it and listen carefully to the answers.

CREATIVITY AND PERSPECTIVE

The real key to creative thought is changing your perspective about a situation. We all have filters. Immanuel Kant is one of the most famous philosophers of the Enlightenment period, and one of his most celebrated works is the "Critique of Pure Reason," where he explains his view of the world and how we come to know things about it. In it he argues against skeptics who said that when you perceive things, you are never really perceiving the actual thing itself, but instead you are only perceiving the *ideas* in your head of what that thing is like. As such, the skeptics argued, because there is sort of a gap between the actual world (the *noumena*) and the image inside your head (the *phenomena*), that image of what the world is like could be completely different to what the world is really like.[iii] Our filter shapes our perceptions of the world and the very way we think. What we hear, touch, feel, and see, and therefore, what we think is filtered through our perspective. The perspective of a single mother in Atlanta is radically different than that of an imam living in Iran or an elderly man living in Canada. Our perspectives shape how we see the world around us, so changing our perspective is what we need to change our thinking. This is easier said than done sometimes, so we must be conscious about approaching this.

Falsify Trauma

Earlier we discussed the *River of our Experience* and how we get used to patterns in our thinking. As we experience stimulus, we tend to automatically file it in the same way, using the same learned patterns. Over time, *The River* carves a deeper and deeper path into the "hillside" of our mind, making it harder to innovate. To change the path of the water on the hillside of our mind, we need to "traumatize" it with a mudslide—or use heavy earth-moving equipment. That would allow the water to flow differently. For our thoughts to flow differently. The key to building up a

---

iii http://www.mrhoyestokwebsite.com/WOKs/Reason/Useful%20Information/Noumenal%20&%20 Phenomenal.htm

resiliency to the *River of our Experience* is to falsify regular *small* traumas, like how a mudslide or earthquake would "shift" the landscape, creating new paths for the water to flow (but in a far less devastating way). Falsifying small traumas is the key to building resiliency and readiness for innovation. This allows us to be ready for change and helps us change our perspective more easily on events and the world around us.

Plants that are intentionally stressed during growth and development do better at surviving in the real world. In reforestation efforts after forest fires, the plants that are most successful come from greenhouses where they intentionally "stress" the plants with abiotic factors such as drought and temperature variations.[iv]

Compare that to a greenhouse-grown houseplant being placed outside for the first time. These plants have a tough time adapting to the outdoor environment. Plants grown in controlled environments and given plenty of nutrients and ideal conditions might be able to flower more or grow larger, but when placed in adverse conditions, such as the outdoors, they will likely flounder and die.

This is also true for us to a certain degree. Those of us who rely on life without change to build our ideal greenhouse conditions miss the chance to become more resilient and readier for innovation. By falsifying small traumas, we can learn to engage our readiness and become more aware. This hyperawareness is important to rethinking how we look at the world and is a key element of shifting our perspective—unlocking our creativity.

One example is our drive to work. Typically, people may try a few different routes when moving to a new place before deciding on what they believe to be the most efficient route. After that, most people tune out on the way to work and it becomes an automatic part of daily life. Does that sound familiar? Is your daily commute roughly the same every day? But then one day there is unexpected construction or a detour. Then we start paying attention. We curse our luck and mutter obscenities under our breath. We adapt to deal with the situation. We become hyperaware. That's because this is a small false trauma. It doesn't devastate us, but it makes us aware of new paths, new surroundings—and we take notice. We take notice of a new part of the world, and it helps us become more resilient.

Small false traumas include anything that shakes up our routine, such as trying a new dish or drink, traveling to a new location, experiencing a different culture, or having a small adventure—anything that intentionally disrupts the *River of our Experience*. These do not need to be big. Even a small, but dramatic, change in wardrobe or our patterned behavior can create micro-resiliency in our attitude about change and prepare us to deal with any actual trauma. This small, false trauma will help shift our phenomena and look at the noumena in an unusual way.

---

iv http://www.greenhousegrower.com/production/plant-culture/stress-is-good-for-plants/

Do one small false trauma for today: Wear red socks. Lie on your back and stare at the ceiling. Eat ice cream for breakfast. Write a poem at midnight. Stand outside in freezing weather for three minutes. Take a new way home from work. It doesn't need to stress you out, but it needs to be intentionally different. Write down what your false trauma will be and share with a few others. Pay attention to what changes. What do you notice that was new?

Childlike Wonder

To be more creative, the simple, elegant, sticky truth is that we need to approach the world with more childlike wonder. Children are constantly learning, and they are already resilient to small traumas. Think about it: Every day they are learning something new, so it is not unusual for them to have filters that are radically different than our "fully formed" adult minds.

At heart, they see with a different lens than adults, and their filter isn't fully formed yet. They haven't had the "why" trained out of them, so they often see solutions to problems that adults don't. They can change perspectives easier because their filter isn't finished being formed. This is because adults tend to assume more about our world as we learn more, and therefore we become further constrained by that which we already "know" to be true. Kids are not constrained in the same way because they do not make the same assumptions. We must let go of what we *know* to be true to make room for that which we *wish* to be true. Kids are excellent at doing this.

Kids can create a stream of new thoughts that adults will automatically skip over because of what they *know*. Kids can easily believe the flying car is not only possible, but obvious. Kids delight in the world around them, making them naturally curious. Adults should mirror this behavior. Ask why and be curious; engage your "kid brain" next time you have a problem that requires creative solutions. At a minimum, children (five- to eight-years old is the ideal age to model) will help you think differently about your problem. Their answers may be simplistic, but sometimes it's just about moving off start to get going, and kids can give you entirely new avenues to think about or confirm ideas you're having.

My daughter was a great sounding board on several projects and reminded me how to build fun and interactivity—she helped my design thinking on an electric vehicle charging station project, an urban streetscape project and a competitive community grant program. Kids keep it fun and make it easier to see the big picture.

Remember, when working with kids, it's important to set the stage in terms they can understand and not constrain their thinking with too much of the dynamic or rules. Just see where they go with it. Ice cream, juice, or sugar of some sort is usually a great facilitation tool as well. See if one of their ideas could work. Many times, kids can help break the creative logjam.

You see, at its core, thinking like a kid is all about learning to change our perspective again. This regular change in perspective helps us reshape our filter and how we work with the *River of our Experience*.

> *CHALLENGE:*
> *Next time you have a problem that needs a creative solution, see if you*
> *can talk with a few kids, explain the idea in clear and simple terms,*
> *and ask them what they would do. Don't argue with their answers; just*
> *consider them and see if you can force connections to your concept or*
> *idea later. Encourage a discussion about why or how they came up with*
> *the ideas. This has the added benefit of helping kids learn to be more*
> *creative and encourages their ability to stay flexible and innovative.*

Creativity Comes In Waves

I don't know why this is true; it just is. Creativity comes in waves. So be prepared to ride that creativity wave as long as you can when it comes. When you get into a place where the ideas are flowing more freely, you need to be ready to keep going and continue with your creative process. This typically means ignoring your normal sense of timekeeping and just working with your creativity when it happens. This is also why the way that we traditionally do brainstorming doesn't work for most of us—it ignores when we are creative in favor of convenience for the group. But I'm getting ahead of myself. More about better brainstorming soon.

For me, creativity waves have lasted anywhere from 15 minutes to three days. I usually find the ideas flow faster and it's easier to connect the dots. And yes, have a drink, relax and let it go. What I find is that the better you get at riding these waves, the more frequently they will come and the easier they will become to use. Many times, I find the best way to capture the creativity wave involves brainstorming or mind mapping on a sheet of paper and building on as many ideas as I can, as quickly as I can. Sort of a rapid-fire self-brainstorming event, where I just let it flow as fast as possible into a visual mind map. A mind map is like the image you saw earlier of *Sustainovation*. That's my style, and you need to develop your own for these moments. This may seem like a silly thing to say but learning to recognize and ride your creative wave will change the power and effectiveness of your creative moments.

Force Connections

Another powerful creativity technique is forcing connections. Forcing connections is a very effective way to create new paths of thinking. There are several ways to do this, and each can unlock your creative brain, but the goal with each is to find new pathways and new conduits to connect materials that seem unrelated or unlikely to relate. The idea is that you are forcing your brain to access its creative side. To force connections, we can remix ideas using randomness, related worlds, and a revolution to help turn a corner in our creative thinking.

Randomness

The only rules here are that you must pick a stimulus that is *truly random* and that has nothing to do with the problem, and then *force* a connection to the problem. The more random the item, and the more creative the forced connection, the more interesting the ideas. There is nothing difficult about this one. Write down a problem or idea you're working on. Literally grab an object, the first that you see, and force connections from your key problem or opportunity to the random object. For example, if you're innovating around the flying car, and you look around and see a paper clip, begin to connect the "essence" of the paper clip to the "concept" of the flying car. A paperclip is flexible. It can be launched. Metal is in both. A paper clip curves. Both holds things together. It connects things. And on and on. Do this with a group for five minutes and see what you can generate in terms of connections. Do it with five groups, each with a different random object and see how it reshapes the problem you are trying to examine. Let it get weird and wild. And you can certainly do this exercise on your own, but this one is great with a group.

> **CHALLENGE:**
> *Put ten random, unrelated objects in a bag. Next time you are faced with a problem, reach into the bag and pull out an object and try to force connections between your challenge or opportunity to the object. When you're done, replace the object with something else random, and continue to use the bag to help spur your creativity.*

Related Worlds

Look to other industries and other professionals in your industry. To use an Old West analogy, you can't keep prospecting in the same old vein and expect to find new gold. Looking at fields related to our own allows us to shift the problem's "rules" and explore a new way of looking at things. For example, if you're in the water distribution department, why not look to see how a water park would handle an issue like yours. If you're in the police department, look to other organizations like the military or Boy Scouts. If you do housing for your community, talk to hotel companies about how they would tackle your issue.

• *How can you combine elements of other people's ideas to make one entirely your own?*
• *How can you remix the thoughts to include new elements you had previously left out?*
• *Is there a publication or a newsletter you can subscribe to that will help you collect and disseminate related ideas efficiently?*
• *How can you remaster an old idea of yours that didn't fly in the past?*
• *Did you give credit to those who contributed to your idea?*
• *Have you tried Google? If not, what's the matter with you? Google it!*

Revolution

Taking a situation to the extreme allows us to expand our horizons and create a thought revolution about the possible and improbable, and it helps us build the simplest, and sometimes the most elegant, solutions.

For example, the potato chip was invented in the 1850s by a man named George Crum. The joke was that George's fries were so large and undercooked that following complaints, he decided to slice the potatoes extra thin and cook them in the fryer for far longer. As a result, he created the potato chip. And it was all because he exaggerated his response to a problem and took it to the extreme.

To begin a thought revolution, start by answering questions that require you to think at extremes. There are many questions we can ask ourselves, and don't concern yourself with solving for today's issues or using today's constraints, as much as solving for these hypothetical situations.

CHALLENGE

Next time you have a problem you are working on, try some of these revolution questions designed to spark your imagination. Here are some sample questions you might consider starting with, but you are only limited by your imagination:

How would you solve this problem if you had no resources to do it?

What if you had ten times as many customers? 1000 times as many?

What would happen if it broke?

What would you do if you had unlimited time to work on this idea?

How small could you make it? What if it needed to be 50 times larger?

What if you reversed the process? Build it backwards if you can. Unbuild it.

Nature

Looking at examples of how nature works to create near-perfect defenses, adaptations, predators, and ingenuity is an excellent way to spark creativity. This is called biomimicry. Ask yourself how nature would solve this, or use nature as inspiration, because nature creates elegant solutions.

Velcro was modeled after the burr. In 1941, the Swiss engineer George de Mestral looked at the burrs under a microscope and noticed they contained hundreds of tiny hooks that could catch on loops of hair or clothing. He developed a material based on this and called it Velcro, from the French words "velours," meaning velvet, and "crochet," meaning hook.

The helicopter was originally inspired by the maple seed. Some modern variations of it were inspired by the dragonfly.

Pound for pound, spider silk is significantly stronger than steel.

Echolocation, used by submarines, was inspired by bats.

Noise pollution on Japanese bullet trains can cause headaches. Air pressure builds up in tunnels in sonic waves that are released as the nose emerges with a shotgun-like bang. A 50-foot "nose" for the train was modeled after the kingfisher beak, which eliminated the air pressure and allowed the trains to go faster.

Nature is a fantastic way to get inspired when you need a new way to think about things. Nature has been providing some of history's greatest thinkers with inspiration for millennia, so why not you?

Use Your Senses

See it. Hear it. Do it. There are three main types of learning: visual, auditory, and kinesthetic. When you begin looking at a problem, think about ways you might be able to see it or do it. Spreadsheets with rows of numbers cannot tell the information in a way that is relatable, but a graph can. And there is nothing like seeing a process be performed or playing with a physical item to give you a better sense of how it can change, be improved or reinvented. Aristotle is generally credited with identifying the categories of our five "traditional" senses: sight, hearing, touch, taste, and smell. But many scientists agree there are upwards of 20 senses! Some of these are less obvious, but it begs the question of how many of your senses you use—and how many more you should be using!

See It.

Visualizing elements of our situation will allow us to learn information in a separate way and to see problems in a different light. Look for patterns between data in graphs. Look at an aerial map or video. If I say it was an amazing sunset, you get an image in your head, but if I show you the picture, you can fully appreciate it. See if you can create a visual that captures the essence of what you are trying to understand. When we were turning off streetlights (and subsequently running a streetlight "adoption" program) in Colorado Springs, we used a map of where the lights were being turned off to show the story of the "haves" and the "have nots" that became an important part of our case to turn the lights back on. The visual helped show the message far better than words or data ever could.

Hear It.

Be sure to truly listen to someone and hear their narrative about a situation, concept, or idea. Be sure to really listen and try to understand from them as much about their thoughts as you can. This is a terrific way to connect with the emotion and story of a situation. When we hear what people say and truly listen, we can learn so much about the need and the emotion, and many times we can find out the urgency as well. This will help us to sell the story later as well as implement the concept faster.

Do It.

Just as seeing a picture of a roller coaster can give you some sense of it, but it is nothing like actually riding one! Kinesthetic learning is an important learning type that is often undervalued compared to visual and auditory, but it is critical to ensure we are completely understand the opportunity. "Doing it" helps us learn kinesthetically and allows us to take in information that seeing it or hearing about it can't. In addition, it often provides a great jumping off point for a *Map Follower* to begin to build ideas and can help us shake the *River of our Experience*. If you want to innovate around a process, there is no better way than to do it, just as describing or taking pictures of how to do a Rubik's Cube would provide none of the experience.

Other Senses

When we are babies and toddlers, the second thing we do with something, besides touch it, is put it in our mouths. But can you imagine solving your problems by licking or tasting them first? It sounds crazy, but once we realize that touching hot stoves and licking cats kind of sucks, we begin to focus on only using the less intimate of our senses: sight and sound. Using senses other than sight and sound allows us to experience situations in a unique way and can trigger unique ideas about how the concept can be improved or the problem lessened. In fact, smells can also create some of the most powerful associations and memories, so consider how we can use a smell to create a lasting memory or how a pungent odor may be impacting perception.

What about some of our less-considered senses? Let's explore how those might be used:

- Chronoception (the perception of time) is impacting your project or might impact it.
- Consider how you might change the process to make it more fun.
- Nociception (the perception of pain): How painful is the experience you've created, and can you make it less painful for the customer? Anesthetics is an entire field dedicated to targeting. different pain receptors. Think about the difference between general versus targeted anesthesia and how important that is.
- Equilibrioception (balance) was used to develop field sobriety tests.
- Proprioception (physical orientation) is important when NASA has to design systems and processes that must function correctly regardless of someone's physical orientation.

If we consider that innovation is about shifting our perception, just using sights or sounds is the same as saying we can have a car in any color—as long as it's black. It may be efficient, but it's hardly creative, and it limits the potential for our creativity.

Instead get intentional about using your other senses to help build upon your great ideas and unlock more of your creativity!

> ### ✎ EXERCISE
> Get three jars and fill them with "smells" such as spices, grass, or shaved scented candles. Do not use gas or mace or something stupid— there, you've been warned— just something with a distinct and strong odor. In a brainstorming session, ask a volunteer to close his or her eyes. Have someone open a jar and hold it under their nose and waft the smell towards their nose. Have them describe the smell with two words, without saying the name of the smell, and write that down. Just for fun, have them see if they can guess the actual smells, and see how close they are. Force associations from these "descriptor" words to the problem you are trying to solve or to the idea you are trying to generate. You could do this same concept using tactile tools, such as silk, sandpaper, and rubber—or taste tools like spices.
>
> Next time you have a brainstorming session, include at least one other "atypical" sense in the process, and see if it shifts your *River*.

Choose What to Leave Out

We live in a world of information overload. It is a world with constant flashing, beeping, buzzing, and vibrating. It can be hard with so much information streaming at us to get our collective selves in gear. Inherently, we can get "writer's block," not from a lack of information, but from far too much. One way to get over a creative block is to put intentional limitations on ourselves.

One notable example of how leaving information out can work is Dr. Suess. After his rampant commercial success with the 225-word *The Cat in the Hat*, Dr. Suess's publisher, Bennett Cerf, bet him "$50 that you can't write a book using only 50 words." He knew that Seuss had used a whopping 225 words in *The Cat in the Hat*, and he knew how Seuss had struggled with that one, so the $50 seemed like easy money. Seuss wrote Green Eggs and Ham, one of the most popular children's book of all time, with only 50 words.[v]

Another example is Usain Bolt, the fastest man in the world. He has never run a mile. Proudly and boastfully, he has never run a whole mile. He chose running a mile to be irrelevant to whether he can run 100 meters well. And he's clearly right. But conventional thinking doesn't follow that logic. Stamina is encouraged where none is required. But it is ultimately irrelevant to the task at hand, as Usain Bolt has demonstrated, and he left it out, allowing him to focus on doing what he's best at: running short distances.

Choosing what information to leave out forces us to clean up our thinking about the problem. Just like a story problem from high school or the SAT's, there is often

---

v https://www.politico.com/story/2013/09/ted-cruz-10-facts-about-green-eggs-and-ham-097332

extra information we don't need to solve the problems constantly coming at us. Tuning out information allows us to focus more attention on a few key facts without being distracted by extraneous information. It is critical that we are solving for the right problem before deciding what to leave out, but then ignoring unnecessary information helps us focus our minds on the problem at hand.

✐ EXERCISE

Write down all the things you are working on in your personal and professional life. Determine which are the top 10. These could be based on time, money, effort, or preference. It does not need to be in order; just write the top ten things. You choose.

How many of these items are you doing well right now?

Narrow the list to only the top three things if you could only have three. Do you think you could do just these three things well? Does this list of priorities match with how you spend your time? If not, why not? What could you leave out?

Consider how you might constrain yourself next time you are being creative to limit the amount of information or simplify the solution to make it easier. This will help you focus your efforts on solving the right problem and creating simpler, and oftentimes more elegant, offerings.

Be Mindful

In our digital age of instant attention, the constant information and sensory overload smartphones produce creates "a relentless need to immediately review and respond to each and every incoming message, alert or ping."[vi] This in turn raises our stress levels and forces us into a near-constant state of "fight or flight," which inhibits our creativity. Being mindful is a wonderful way to shut down the noise, the brain, and the information, and just "be." Taking even a few minutes to do this every day will allow you to shut down the adrenaline response of information overload and free up your brain to accept information and increase creativity.

✐ EXERCISE

Set a timer for two minutes and shut your eyes. Just focus on your breathing. Breathing in and out. Deeply. Slowly. Feel the air enter your lungs and exhale your lungs. Calm your mind and focus on breathing in and out. Then be silent for the remainder of the two minutes.

Do you feel calmer? Do you feel more capable of processing information? This can take some practice, as it's counter to our normal daily behavior in many cases.

---

vi http://www.everydayhealth.com/emotional-health/0112/your-smartphone-may-be-stressing-you-out.aspx?xid=tw_everydayhealth_20120112_smartphone

Get The Blood Pumping

Movement and exercise can get our minds working in innovative ways. Even stepping away from the desk for a few minutes to take a short walk can reframe an idea you're working on. Or get outside and throw a Frisbee—my personal favorite. Or do some pushups or bounce on an exercise ball. Whatever it is, exercise and movement are a fantastic way to get your creative juices going.

Engaging in activity in a social way also allows us to collaborate better with kinesthetic learners—people who are primarily activated by "doing" an activity. These people tend to feel more comfortable expressing themselves when they are engaged in a physical activity at the same time. This includes things as simple as twirling a pen, but it can include things as rigorous as exercise. Remember that we all express ourselves differently and that finding better ways to open people's creativity is the goal.

Beyond inviting different learning styles, there are many reasons to exercise for better innovation. First, it improves your memory. A 2016 report in *Current Biology*[vii] describes that exercise after an activity can help you retain the task over the long term. Second, it increases your energy. Men who cycled for 20 minutes reported a 166 percent increase in self-reported energy levels compared with only 15 percent for those who did not. Exercise also has benefits of staving off depression, curbing cravings, reducing risks of serious cancers, and other mind-body benefits.[viii] In short: exercise is good.

And while exercise is one way to get it done, stretching, movement, or *anything* to get the blood flowing is generally a safe way to get restarted while resting and reinvigorating our minds at the same time. When we are focused on moving we are not focused on our problems. Focus your senses on how you "feel" when you are moving and not on the problem in your head. Even a brief respite can help you think more clearly. Get up and stand with your back against the wall. Jump on one foot. Swing your arms wildly over your head. Lie on your back and pop up quickly and jump as high as you can! Make it fun and ridiculous, but get up and get moving—you might just find your creativity unleashed!

Sniglets

A *Sniglet* is any word that should be in the dictionary but isn't. *Sniglet*izing is all about making up your own words as a way of re-expressing an idea. *Sniglet*izing is fun and is a fantastic way to shape how we look at our problems. Re-expressing how we look at problems can help us find innovative ways of thinking about them. Even the meaning of the word innovation has undergone a fundamental shift in meaning over time. In the 1980s, Rich Hall coined the term *Sniglet* in a comedy routine, but the

---

vii http://www.cell.com/current-biology/fulltext/S0960-9822%2816%2930465-1
viii Time July 4, 2016 pg. 18

truth is there is a lot of power in making up your own words. In fact, some of you might have even had *Sniglet* books as a kid. Here are a few fun examples.

- *Bovilexia:* the uncontrollable urge to lean out the car window and yell "moo" at cows as you pass.
- *Sustainovation:* creating sustainable innovation.
- *Elecelleration:* the mistaken belief that the more you press the elevator button the faster it arrives.

While *Sniglets* are a wonderful way to have some fun and add levity, the concept is quite important. Words have power. They shape how we think and how we perceive, influence, and understand the world around us. Finding a new way to think about problems requires novel words. *Sniglets* are a fantastic way to take control of the creativity conversation because words have power. Our words and our vocabulary influence our perceptions and ability to think.

Several studies have supported the fact that the way we use words can shape our perceptions and abilities. Changing our perceptions and harnessing our abilities is what unleashing creativity is all about. And in the end, words that we currently know are just great mnemonic devices for objects, thoughts, actions, feelings, etc. We also simplify by using acronyms, another mnemonic device where the "words" created are memorable: LOL, FAQ, OMG, SCUBA, FYI, and TGIF are just a few. Creating words that better suit our needs for conveying objects, thoughts, actions, or feelings helps us take control of solving problems creatively.

In a paper published in 2008, MIT cognitive neuroscientist Michael Frank and colleagues demonstrated that Pirahã, a language spoken by a small Amazonian community, has no number words at all. They have words for "around one," "some," and "many." Researchers asked the Pirahã to count spools in one bucket and make an equal number of balloons. The Pirahã would do fine when they could lay out spools and match up balloons, but if they were given a bucket of 17 spools and could count them, but were not allowed to lay them out, they failed nearly every time. This is because they did not have a means to count. They had no number words.[ix]

Think about this for a second. It makes sense but is likely something you have never given another thought to. Imagine having no way to count out change or exchange large numbers of goods precisely. Math is irrelevant if you cannot count, and how different would life be without math? We would be in the dark ages—just like this tribe.

We also use words to remember complex concepts so that we might be able to recall them later, even if we couldn't "explain" them easily, such as with calculus. This allows us to look the concept up later and "re-learn" it—because we know it exists.

---

ix http://www.scientificamerican.com/article/does-language-shape-what/

The words we use and the order we use them in can fundamentally change people's perception of an idea, and this is incredibly important during implementation.

As an example, "door" and "portal" are synonyms, but the images they conjure in our mind and our reaction to these words is likely very different. A door likely evokes something that is standard issue and plain—a rectangular and boxy thing, maybe with a window, maybe with a brass knob or handle. Nothing too fancy. But portal—portal is something very different entirely. It is the entrance to a new universe, a round hobbit-like door or something of radical design, ornate, and opening to a place altogether surreal. As we can see, while they are similar in meaning and could technically be words substituted for each other, the way we visualize them and *experience* them is quite different.

Another fitting example is the word "sustainability." As someone with a personal passion for our planet (it's our only one, after all), I was stunned by how many people in a conservative community like Colorado Springs equate the word "sustainability" with "liberalism," not "conservation," which is at the core of conservative principles. But as you can see, for skeptics of human-made climate change in a hyper-partisan era of politics it is a lightning rod word in a conservative community that will paralyze further discussion. I have learned there are distinct types of conservatives: fiscal, religious, and military. There are likely other "types," but these are the three most predominant, and each has their own language. Finding a new way to approach this conversation about protecting our planet is critical to being effective if you believe in "sustainability." Each of these conservative types has their own language. Conservation (at the core of conservative principles) seems to resonate with fiscal conservatives, stewardship (a biblical term) with religious conservatives, and resilience (emergency management) with military conservatives. That meant that when I would speak with these groups about "sustainability" projects, I would adjust my language to ensure my audience would hear the message I needed them to. *Sniglets* let us control the definition and therefore the perception. And yes, there are liberal languages as well.

We can inspire people with how we speak, or turn them off, and when we are trying to build momentum and support, inspiring people, or at the very least not turning them off, is a critical part of success, so consider your language carefully, because words have immense power. So, take back the power of words and their influence on your creative process and consider using *Sniglets* to change your paradigm!

⌀ EXERCISE

Develop your own *Sniglet*. Think about your biggest pet peeve or something silly that doesn't have a name or a product that should be invented. Smash related words together in combinations to get started. Develop your word, then write it down and give it a definition and share it with others! See if you can get your *Sniglet* trending on Twitter or as part of your office vernacular.

Parting Thoughts...

Building and growing creativity in ourselves and our teams is about practicing skills that shift our perspective—things that falsify trauma and allow us to push our personal boundaries. The *River of our Experience* is a powerful force to fight against and it takes practice on skills that likely will make us uncomfortable, but if we get better at pushing our boundaries, we can find new depths of our creativity and ride a new wave to better, more innovative ideas.

GROWING IDEAS

There are many techniques for growing great ideas, and learning how to facilitate successful group brainstorming sessions just allows us to multiply the effect of our creativity. But we also need to be sure we are setting ourselves up for success with this process by finding the right facilitator, developing the right rules, and encouraging the right environment for our process.

Let's acknowledge right now that the concept of the miracle one-hour brainstorming session solving our problems is ludicrous. Yes, ludicrous. If you haven't already noticed, this process has several serious flaws.

First, it promotes the loud and ill-considered idea to the forefront. If your idea happens outside the one-hour session, sorry, no dice. Because of that, it encourages the dreaded "meeting after the meeting" where decisions *really* get made. In some cases, this happens because the ideation process left creative people feeling like they had more to say—a natural result of their personal creative timelines catching up to them. This process also dampens the voice of people who need time to consider or weigh information—more analytical or thoughtful personalities. It is honestly a miracle that any clever ideas are generated from this kind of slap-dash process at all, as it is based largely on the individual and not on the group's ability to harness and multiply ideas. Yet this "one-hour brainstorm" technique for ideation is far and away the most popular technique I see most organizations use to solve problems and generate innovative ideas. To effectively brainstorm and grow ideas, we need to set up a fertile environment.

When we have the right environment, we can grow the best ideas, so let's get set up for success.

Finding The Facilitator

The right facilitator is critical to the ideation process being successful. This person does not have to be the boss, nor should that be a condition to be the process leader. The boss is not the facilitator by default. In fact, leveling the playing field by taking the "power of the pen" from the boss and requiring the team to show dedication to the process means the environment is more fertile for ideas. Regardless of who leads, choose someone who is good about inviting people into the conversation, who can command respect, and who is empowered to keep the conversation moving. The facilitator's role is to accomplish the agreed-upon goal of the group, not to know it all. Facilitating is not for everyone, so be sure to pick the right person for the job, and if you don't have someone skilled on your team, find someone from another team who is, because the facilitator is critical to the success of any brainstorming process. Good facilitation has been my bread and butter for many years and is a critical part of my ideation success. Working to encourage and extract ideas from a group is scientific art—and it is a powerful art if you practice it.

As a general guideline, here are some basics of good facilitation from Viv McWaters, a renowned professional facilitator, who has provided as good an overview as anything I've seen:[x]

1. Capture information in people's own words

2. Encourage participation

3. Be comfortable with silence

4. Give instruction clearly and briefly

5. Build independence of the group

6. Avoid leading the group or the discussion

7. Set the context for the meeting

8. Create a welcoming space

9. Take care of time and mind the pace

10. Self care. Take care of yourself

Setting The Stage

Personally, I like to get introductions out of the way and do some sort of icebreaking activity, depending on how well the team knows each other. Hopefully, we can establish that this will be laid back and fun and set up the environment for success— bathrooms, water, free food (always a winner), massage chair, frozen yogurt machine, etc. Just kidding, but you get the idea.

Check the environment. The temperature of the room should be cool, but not cold, to keep people alert. There needs to be space for people to move around. Be sure you have the supplies you need, such as large sticky pads, sticky notes, markers, a

x http://vivmcwaters.com.au/2012/11/17/10-basic-group-facilitation-skills/

white board—whatever works for your needs. Make sure you have whatever it is that your team needs to be successful.

Building The Rules

Once we have the intros done, I suggest building ground rules and expectations that the room can agree to. Write them down for all to see. If it is a particularly difficult or contentious room, or if the people in the room are at various levels of the organization, ask them to sign a document stating that they are "buying in" to the ground rules. This gives us the ability to refer to the ground rules during the process and ensure they are being followed.

Here are some ground rules that I like to use or suggest at the start of a brainstorming process:

- "Live at the edges." Ask those who are typically extroverted to listen more and those who are introverted to speak more.
- "Respect is a right." Disagreeing about an idea is great, but it must be done respectfully. Talk about positions, not people. Talk about processes, not individuals.
- "No ranks in the room." This means that all people are equal in the eyes of brainstorming. There are no hierarchical relationships in the room, and everyone is approached as an equal. Great ideas come from everyone, not just the boss.
- "Fall out of love with your idea." More on this to come, but open your mind to workable solutions other than the one you've come up with. Fall out of love with your idea as being the only fix.
- "Be respectful of time." This gives you permission to move the brainstorming along if people get stuck on an issue, and it allows the facilitator to keep the conversation moving—in the interest of time.
- "Vote with your feet." If you're not finding value, you don't want to be here, or you think it's not for you, feel free to leave. No one will think less of you, but if you are in the room, you are engaged with the process. And yes, I have had people get up and leave—and that's okay.
- "Electronics diet." Cell phones go on airplane mode or sleep mode. If you need to look at your phone or make a call or text, please exit the room or wait until our breaks.

Once the list is generated, have the room agree to abide by the rules, sign a document if necessary, and post the rules for all to see. Use these rules as a gentle reminder to draw out thoughts and comments from those people who are less comfortable and to gently shut down people who are too opinionated or verbose. Use your rights as the facilitator to make sure all voices are heard through the brainstorming process.

Starting With Seeds

To start any session, we must begin by defining the goal. What is it we want to accomplish or address with this brainstorming session, and what does success look like? Write the goal down very clearly for all to see. It is the facilitator's job to keep the session moving in that direction. Consider this tilling the field so we can start planting the right seeds.

Once we know what kind of plants we want to grow (goals), we can begin using our creativity techniques to challenge the room to generate great ideas. Wild ideas. Uncomfortable ideas. Fun ideas. Stupid ideas. We need to plant as many seeds as possible to increase our chances for success. Spend at least half of the meeting time generating ideas. Use the creativity techniques you've already learned to force connections or to use all your senses—whatever works for your room. Have the room split into teams to generate ideas and then present to each other. Have the team exchange ideas and work on each other's ideas. There is no right way to do this, and anything that keeps it flowing is a good thing. And now that you've planted all these seeds, it's time for something that almost nobody does: give the ideas time to grow. Wrap up the meeting, and ask the team to consider the ideas and see if anything else comes to them over the next week.

You see, when growing ideas, we need to have some space and time to let the ideas germinate. We need to take time between brainstorming "sessions" to give the team time to consider the solutions, outcomes, or ideas of the initial session. To take the analogy one step further, consider a situation where you are planting seeds, only you don't know which will be flowers and which will be weeds. You need to plant them all to give them time to grow, but if you pull them out before they begin to mature, you will not be able to tell one seedling from another, meaning you are just as likely pluck a weed from the ground as you are to pluck a flower. By giving the ideas a little time to develop, it is much easier to tell which is an innovative idea and which is just cluttering up the landscape. We may inadvertently pluck out the best idea if we start pulling out ideas too early. We need to grow them for a while first. That's why it is critical for *every* idea, no matter how ridiculous it may seem, to make the board during brainstorming.

A few years ago, a city in the Netherlands had a real problem with litter. A once-clean section of town had become an eyesore because of people littering. Because it was a prominent neighborhood, the community formed a committee to deal with the issue. During the initial brainstorming sessions, people threw out ideas like doubling the fine for litter, increasing enforcement in the area, and even rewarding people for keeping it clean. This last idea got little support and was quickly dismissed as infeasible and silly—it was plucked.

As a result, the committee recommended doubling the fine from 25 guilders to 50 guilders, and the local government enacted the recommendation. Over the next few months, there was negligible impact. Not surprisingly, the people who were littering weren't the most civically-minded folks around, so the fine increase made virtually no impact. The committee reconvened, and instead of redoing the brainstorming process, they took the time to revisit and explore the previous list of ideas a little further, and they decided maybe rewarding people wasn't so crazy after all.

This time the committee decided to brainstorm how to reward people for keeping the area clean and came up with an idea: install a device in the trash cans that would play a silly joke when people lifted the can lid up. It was an instant hit, and people, especially kids, were cleaning up the area just to hear the jokes. A few months later, the neighborhood was noticeably cleaner. In this case, it was hard to tell which idea was the flower and which was the weed because the fledgling idea was plucked too soon.

The reason all ideas make the board is so we can ensure we see the full spectrum of creativity of the team, allow us time to process what we see and hear, ensure our team members feel heard, and document great ideas in case we accidentally choose the weed instead of the flower.

Voices Are Like Spices

Each situation is different, but I find it helpful to remember that voices are very much like spices, and every room has some spicier people than others. Sometimes we only need a little bit of a spice for it to be effective, and sometimes we need a lot more. Just because a person is quiet doesn't mean they don't have great ideas. Or vice versa. In a brainstorming session, it is important to have a facilitator who recognizes how to draw out the voices of everyone in the room and to keep a balance about how the voices are heard. Be aware that some people are not fans of being silenced, but they can transform the process if not held in check. The rules should help enforce this. As a facilitator, being mindful of who is contributing too much and who is not contributing enough is an important part of a high-functioning brainstorming environment—and part of the art of facilitation. This requires practice and is often one of the most challenging aspects of learning facilitation.

Being The Best Brainstormer

So how can your team be the best idea-generating team it can be? First, stop being so in love with your own idea! It's only natural; I mean, *you* came up with it, and you're clearly the most brilliant person in the room. In all sincerity, it's not too hard to let happen, but it can be detrimental to the process. Feeling like you *know* the answer before walking into the room is a recipe for disaster. During brainstorming, it is necessary to fall out of love with an idea. But during implementation, it is necessary to fall into love with one.

I love an idea introduced in the book *Sticky Wisdom:*[xi] To grow great ideas, we need to add more SUN and less RAIN. SUN stands for Suspend, Understand, and Nurture.

RAIN is React, Assume, and INsist. When we hear someone else's idea, remember to Suspend your reaction for two minutes and not React; Understand the idea by asking clarifying questions, don't Assume anything; and Nurture the ideas by using "and" to build on the idea, not INsisting there is only one way to do it, or using the word "but" to tear it down.

These techniques to use more SUN and less RAIN on your ideas will help you be a great participator in the process as well as provide a great guideline for your team to use when ideating together.

Fall Out of Love

As someone walking into a brainstorming meeting, we need to fall out of love with our own idea. Falling out of love is necessary. Walking in with pre-conceived notions or being locked into an idea inhibits our ability to be open to other ideas. As we discussed, it is hard to determine what is a flower and what is a weed without giving ideas time to grow.

Be sure to bring your idea up and put it forward, including potential advantages and disadvantages, but become disconnected from the desire to have your idea be the "right" outcome. This can be hard to do, as sometimes we have an emotional connection to our idea. But how could our counterparts possibly feel comfortable contributing to the stable of ideas, if they must fear upsetting us by disagreeing? Also, there are very often many "right" outcomes, so let's not allow arrogance to cloud our judgment.

Slow Down To Go Fast

To create ideas that are truly the best ideas possible, take additional time during the brainstorming process to identify and build better ideas. This means having two different sessions when we brainstorm, not just one. This is an adjustment from how we typically do meetings. That's why I advocate for using *two different sessions* to brainstorm. Plan this into the process. The first one is about getting ALL ideas on the board, then using some directed discussion and voting to develop them, and if necessary, narrow the field to the most impressive, efficient, or creative ideas for follow up. Clarify what ideas are still on the table and ask the team to come prepared to discuss these ideas further in a week so you can narrow down the path going forward. Encourage people to generate and send you ideas if they feel strongly that something needs to be considered, giving the quieter and more reserved people in the room a chance to be heard.

I would argue *most* people are not built for the rapid fire and extroverted world of one-hour office brainstorming. It is critical to give people time to consider ideas,

xi Sticky Wisdom: How to Start a Creative Revolution at Work by ?WhatIf!

Sustainovation o– 42 –o *Growing Ideas*

because these people are often considerate and deliberate about their thinking and can sometimes see connections others can't. I'm sure you know people who are brilliant but not loud. By generating ideas in one session, allowing people to process the concepts for a few days, and then holding a session to revisit the ideas and "complete" the brainstorming, we help engage more people's creativity. It allows everyone to ride their personal creativity wave—when they have it, not when we *want* them to have it. We allow people to consider workable solutions and help develop more flowers and fewer weeds. We slow it down so that when we do develop an idea, it is the right one, making it easier to implement. Not all ideas will be flowers using this technique, but you will end up with a lot fewer weeds.

Compile the complete list of ideas, and start the discussion at the second brainstorming meeting by reminding the team how you got to this point and what the goal is: to determine the best path forward and develop a pilot and action plan. Put forward any new ideas that came in to the group during the break between sessions (send it out in advance) and facilitate discussion among the group about where people think the best solution is. Use voting stickers to narrow the topics, so you can have a focused discussion on only a few options, and see if any present themselves as viable solutions. If necessary, ask people to develop the ideas further, but typically it is possible to get to a limited, but reasonable, set of solutions to pursue, pilot, and grow. Don't just assume one solution is what you should pursue—can two or three ideas be reasonably pursued simultaneously to create a pipeline of success?

Fall In Love

After the brainstorming is done and the idea is selected, it's time to fall in love with it. Hopefully, by generating ideas together, giving people time to think about them, and then revisiting them, you will develop more successful concepts with greater buy-in. Then it's time to get the team excited about the concept and *their* role in its success. Get the team talking about the *compelling why* statement, the elevator pitch for the project, and the value proposition. That sets the stage for successful implementation, and support throughout the implementation process by the entire team.

I find a *Sniglet*, clever turn of phrase, acronym, or great branding can really energize a group of people and inject some love into the idea as a quick win. "Steal the Styrofoam," "FitBitters: A Bit Fit FitBit Challenge," "The Shareway," "iFun," and the VIPER program are all examples of fun program names generated by a team, and more times than I can count, an excellent brand has given a much-needed boost of momentum to a fledgling program. This also gets people curious, which is a great chance to start a dialogue about your idea and refine your elevator pitch.

If there are some who are not on board, talk with them separately. Find out their objections, and make sure to note those, as they may arise again and make a great space to prepare for in future discussions. See if you can persuade them to see your point of view. Don't push; just inquire. If they aren't on board, don't force anything;

simply thank them for their participation in the process. The goal is not to get them on board with the idea, but to ensure they won't lie down on the tracks in front of the progress train and stop it. And if their objections or concerns turn out to be correct, hopefully the team will be more prepared to face those challenges. Our goal at this point is to get as many people on board with the idea as we possibly can.

We Don't Know It All

We don't know it all. Admitting that is half the battle. Now ask for help.

As we approach implementation of a creative idea or problem set, it is important for us to know what we do and do *not* know about the key aspects of delivering a project concept. There are many people out there who might know more on a topic than we do, so invite them in! We can tell people the key elements of the idea and have them help us connect the dots on how to best accomplish the larger concept.

This process builds buy-in over the course of the brainstorming and allows subject-matter experts to weigh in. It also allows us to not shoulder the burden alone and minimizes hard feelings from not being included in the process. We want everyone to have ownership in the innovation's success. Admitting we don't know it all can be a tricky thing to do for some people, but projects often fail because the people who have the knowledge weren't consulted early on—or at all in—the project development. We might miss the best, most effective path forward if we assume we know it all and don't invite the right players at key moments.

Our organization's practitioners are the key to connecting the dots and can help a program succeed faster. The people doing the work know the sounds of the engine, the nuances of the systems, the way it would impact our customers, and what could make it faster. Be sure to involve these practitioners early and often.

Parting Thoughts...

To truly multiply our creative brainpower, we need to set up our environment for success. By creating separate brainstorming sessions, getting a strong facilitator, putting the right people in the room, setting some ground rules and encouraging all ideas to make the board, we can ensure we have fertile soil to plant ideas. By applying creativity techniques in a collaborative environment, we can generate innovative ideas and narrow them down to the very best for implementation!

PILOT. PILOT. PILOT.

By that I don't mean that you should fly every project. I mean that now that you have an idea, it's time to develop the pilot project and let it fly. The pilot project, or "pilot," is a powerful innovation tool and a part of building *Sustainovation*. Pilot everything. Pilots are one of the keys to innovation success. A pilot project is a smaller-scale version of a larger innovation concept. Pilots are limited in scope and scale. They are not designed to be permanent. Pilots allow us to be successful in implementing an idea and help people feel less threatened by a concept. If done *correctly*, pilots never fail. Yes, you read that right. Pilots never fail.

During my career, I launched, or was a key partner, in 65 first-of-their-kind pilot projects. These projects ranged from massive biofuel and alternative energy programs to office supply reuse swaps. Some were wildly successful. Some were not. But none of them were true failures in my eyes.

The reason pilots don't fail is that they allow us to test ideas and learn lessons, and *that* is where our commitment must be. Pilots are all about *trying*—and that's the point: We can't fail if we *try in the right ways*, we learn from the experience, and we try again. We may not get the results we want or expect every time, but we try, and that is part of how successful innovation happens—courage, persistence, testing, iterating, improving. That is how we get good at innovating—testing out pilot projects.

Pilots allow us to demonstrate whether an idea will work (or not), change the concept, approach or implementation, and try again. Pilots give us the chance to win others over. *Or* to learn that an idea does *not* work as expected and shouldn't continue, in which case we have avoided the risk of a failed system-wide implementation by testing it first. Therefore, pilots never fail.

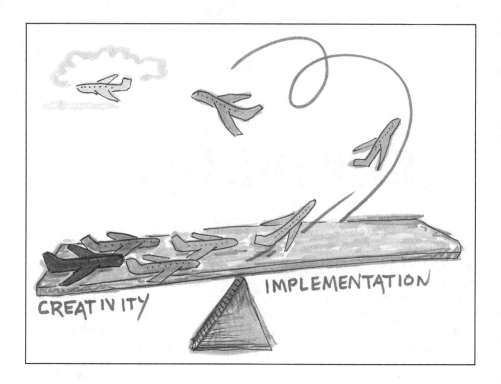

Pilots are where creativity turns into implementation. Pilots are how most great innovation happens. People build a prototype or implement the process in their work group, see what works and what doesn't, improve it, and do it all over again. As an inventor, Edison made 1,000 unsuccessful attempts at inventing the light bulb. When a reporter asked, "How did it feel to fail 1,000 times?" Edison replied, "I didn't fail 1,000 times. The light bulb was an invention with 1,000 steps." Our goal is to construct a pilot with the best information we have available in a way so that it collects the maximum amount of valid data about our idea with the minimum level of effort.

This allows us to keep costs low, time commitments limited, and fear of change muted.

The Tipping Point

Pilots are incredibly important in government. They allow us to tip the system in favor of the innovator—in favor of *Sustainovation*. We need to set the stage and frame pilot projects as "trying." They should start small enough to test an idea and give us room as innovators to try, even when there is resistance. Trying allows us to create innovation space, even if it's just a little at first. It allows us to change the conversation from change-resistant to "I'm trying"—and "you're not." When we create space in the organization to try out pilot projects, we unwittingly give others permission to try as well. This starts the right kind of innovation conversation and allows innovation to spiral up.

Be honest about what works and what doesn't. Build trust with people, and slowly expand the size of projects you pilot, and when you start to get wins that are more recognized throughout the organization, it creates innovation space for everyone.

One example is when we built the award-winning Impact|Adams training and development program. We volunteered to take over a program that was steadily losing employee interest (75 percent loss in attendees over the previous 12-year period) and needed revitalization. Our county manager agreed and allowed us to attempt a program realignment. Training and development is a key recruitment, service delivery, and retention tool for organizations, so we had a silent crisis on our hands. The program we inherited included mostly "anti" trainings (violence in the workplace, sexual discrimination, etc.), and some basic leadership training. There was very limited technical training and any "soft skills" training was primarily taught by HR staff only. So, we reorganized and brought in people who were passionate trainers to oversee the program. And yes, we reduced the budget in the process by reducing contracted coaching services, finding offsets, and realigning existing staff. We focused our Impact|Adams efforts on three things: Evolve|U (comprehensive training), Develop|Us (mentoring and coaching), and We|Care (volunteerism). We piloted and iterated nearly every aspect of the existing program, partnering with our employees to develop employee trainers, increasing the number and frequency of training offerings, and offering electives that improved our employees' morale as well as their technical, soft, and interpersonal skills. We found subject-matter experts among our employees and activated them (stress reduction taught by an employee who teaches yoga, etc.). We dramatically increased availability of online offerings. We prepared employees to grow in their careers through training and development tracks for employees. We created "hack your life" videos that were two-minute employee videos about making life easier. We tracked data about the program accurately, completely, and consistently. We created and nurtured our employees through a mentoring program, offered hands-on lean and strengths coaching for work groups, and ran a volunteer program that donated hundreds of hours to the community's non-profits. We created a program that people were excited about, that played to our employees' passions, and that ultimately breathed life into a program that had gone stale. And to do all this, we piloted and learned a *lot*. As a result, we increased the number of people who voluntarily attended training by 67 percent over the previous year, created a 60-person mentoring program, activated 14 new employee trainers, offered 24 new classes, performed over 85 hours of lean and strengths coaching, and our employees volunteered over 400 hours in our community—in one year.

One of my favorite innovations we offered was free training to all Colorado governments, schools, and non-profits. To offer the "free training" concept, my team decided to take the excess space available after our employees had signed up for our top-rated training classes and offer the remainder of the space to the community. Free for all who work to serve our public. A rising tide lifts all boats. A message of passion and purpose that resonated: the capacity for all four free classes was gone in one week over the holidays. Seventeen different outside organizations participated. People were excited by the idea of high-quality, free training that was relevant to them. But as with any pilot, there were unintended consequences, both positive and negative.

Our first pilots showed that people don't value "free," so they are more likely to be a no-show (more than 25 percent in our first round of offerings). Attendees from outside the organization also had incredibly positive interactions with our staff, enriching the experiences of both, and stretching the abilities of our employee teachers in positive ways. It also created positive touch points for our organization with the community. The people who showed up were motivated and were clearly the kind of people we wanted to recruit—and they were asking about working for us. We were contacted by outside paid trainers who saw our program and wanted to offer our employees "free training" if it could be open to others. They wanted access to a wide audience, a venue, and we wanted the highest quality training. We encountered unexpected resistance from inside the organization while the idea was wildly popular externally. There were many unintended consequences of this pilot.

So, we learned. We iterated. We clarified the goal of the program. We learned the class types we should not change and the offerings we should. We offered free classes to our employees and the public from paid trainers who offered pro bono services. We developed goals and metrics about external engagement, training offerings, training quality and turnover. We decided to change a few classes based on feedback. We implemented a no-show policy and expanded the offerings. We increased interactions and touch points, providing a chance to recruit. We gathered information, learned, experimented, and continued to iterate. We used pilots to learn and create a pattern of innovation. And we won the "Outstanding Achievement in Local Government" Award from the Alliance for Innovation for our efforts—allowing us to spread the model of employee-centered training and development to more communities.

Pilots can do the same for everyone. Pilots can unlock the world of opportunity for innovation in any workplace.

"Failure"

We need to rethink how we look at "failure." Failure is a perception that others might have for your projects, but if you embrace the fact that innovation is creativity implemented, you know that innovation is happening with every single pilot—and is less dependent on the result. In innovative communities, they do not dwell on the two pilot projects that didn't work—they get excited about the eight that did. They learn lessons, iterate, improve and grow. They understand and accept that risk is a part of the equation and a pilot project is the tipping point in innovation. It's where we move from idea to innovation. And it's where we learn.

The key to using pilots is to "fail" faster, so you can succeed more often. That's because our ability to succeed is linked to our willingness to fail.

By most people's measures, I fail. *A lot*. But I succeed even more, which takes time. As a serial civic innovator, I have learned from my own experiences, as well as those of my peers, that the key ingredients of being a great innovator are the *willingness* to fail—to fail smart, to fail easy, to fail often, to fail fast, and to fail small. Learning how to be a better "failure" will unlock your success with innovation. But you and I know that every pilot is an innovation and a part of building a culture of innovation. So, the term "failure" is used somewhat tongue-in-cheek here, as "failure" might be how someone else sees a pilot that did not work as you intended. The truth is that piloting is the tipping point for innovation, so the real metric is moving every time you pilot: *permission to try new things*. Who knew being such a colossal "failure" could pay off so much?

Thomas Edison knew. Leonardo da Vinci knew. Both created and piloted and tinkered and revised and kept going. Undaunted and unyielding in their pursuits, they both recognized that admitting it didn't work as planned was a terrific way to create a better plan. And a better one. As we discussed, we must acknowledge that our ability to succeed is intrinsically linked to our willingness to fail. Pilots are the most powerful tool to minimize risk while pushing boundaries. Pilots allow us to aggregate our innovation risk across a portfolio of projects, reducing the impact of any one failure and conditioning the organization for greater risk.

The rest of these pilot techniques minimize the risk that you would be fired for taking risks, and while there are no guarantees when you're pushing boundaries, pilots are about learning how to be more successful in navigating greater risk.

Fail Smart

First, fail smart. Become a learner. Get smarter. Use your knowledge to gain more knowledge. Identify the "gray areas" in your organization and learn about them. What processes or products or services are muddled or are being ignored because there is no clear owner? Exchange knowledge with a peer in another department and learn the language of other workgroups. Talk about the gaps and opportunities that are being missed.

For me, buying fuel turned into knowledge about how a fleet works, giving me a chance to learn about public works and utilities, and then administrative services, performance, etc. And please, regardless of what else you learn, learn about how your organization's budgeting works. How the money moves. What requires approvals and what doesn't. How accounts, expenditure authority, revenues, and transfers work. Read rules and regulations, even though they can be mind-numbingly boring. This allows you to rebuff resistance based in fear, and not fact.

Fail Easy

A pilot is, in the end, about acting. This means that when we cannot agree, we still agree on forward. We try *something*. And we learn, iterate, and adapt. On the fly, if we must. But we reduce the barriers to action. The pilot project will not be perfect, and there are no perfect projects, only perfect plans—so let go of the need to have it all figured out, and act. If it is hard to participate, make it as easy as possible. We just need to test a theory out, so we need participation.

For example, in the Evolve|U example I used earlier, we were uncertain what kind of response we would get for the "free" class offerings. We expected it to be good, but there was no way to tell that, so why create additional barriers for people to access the pilot? So, we only asked for a name, an email, a class selection and an organization type (government, non-profit, school). In the future, we knew we would want more robust information about people attending the classes, but to get started and begin learning, this was enough information to make some next decisions and to keep the process so simple there were virtually no barriers to participation. Consider your pilot project's barriers—lengthy forms, processing, special sign-ins, longer waits, confusing language, technical challenges, etc.—and how you might minimize them.

Fail Often

Generate a pipeline of innovations and use pilots to launch your ideas. Don't just start one pilot, start three or five or ten pilots around a topic as we did with the Impact|Adams example. This way if one of these innovations fails, we have the next idea, iteration, or innovation just around the corner. This allows us to separate ourselves from the risk of any one idea not working and to create a series of small wins, leading to bigger wins. In addition, this will help protect us from haters and *GOWG Syndrome* (more on this later) stopping our project. Because there will always be haters, and sometimes government is just plain slow. Plan for it. It's like that adage: "the best time to plant a tree was twenty years ago. The second-best time is today." It means that whether a project may take three days, weeks, months, or years, start today. Just keep them moving forward by hard-won inches, as time and opportunity allows. By creating a pipeline of pilot projects, we can pilot an idea, move on, and keep the wins coming, even with the occasional hiccup or unsuccessful project.

I have over 65 pilot projects in my government career where I played a significant role in the idea or implementation of the concept. Of those projects, I would say that 83 percent of them produced a result that was successful—some mildly and some wildly. The remaining 17 percent produced sub-par results—and that's okay. If I had a track record of 100 percent success, I couldn't say that I was pushing the boundaries of my abilities hard enough. That means that (roughly) out of every seven pilot projects I work with, I have one that doesn't work. And I can live with that. After every single one of those "failures," I had another pilot project in progress, ready to shift the conversation from "failure" to "success" again. So, consider how you can create a pipeline of pilot projects that are all moving forward, slowly if need be, but moving forward.

Fail Fast

An effective pilot program has a short duration—one month to six months is ideal for most projects. A pilot should be designed for the minimum amount of time we need to prove a concept works—or not. Be sure it is long enough that you can learn from it and make valid conclusions, but generally you want a first pilot project to be as short as possible. Most pilots can be completed in three months—time enough to learn lessons and get to a good *Blame-Free Autopsy* to discuss what worked and what didn't.

 Some pilot projects could last up to a year when making massive system changes, so be sure the pilot reflects the seriousness of the challenge and change ahead. If the undertaking is big, a longer pilot might be warranted. But shorter is better in a pilot, generally speaking.

Fail Small

A small-scale pilot minimizes resistance because it is all about trying something new and allows us to test a concept. Test an internal idea on one work group, one division, or one department. Test an external idea on one section of town, one neighborhood, or one community group. Consider what is the smallest (and fastest) pilot possible that can prove or disprove a concept and get a valid result. We can use this smaller pilot to learn how to build a bigger one. What is great about this is that it allows us to control the variables and understand how they interact so that we can build a bigger second pilot. Which makes sense—our goal isn't to blindly commit to an idea, but to see how it works—that's the commitment we are asking people to make with us: to try ideas. So, keeping pilot projects small (and fast) minimizes resistance, minimizes the impact of change on the organization, and speeds up innovation efforts.

Measure. But Make It Matter.

If we can't measure it, we're not able to change or move the needle on our ideas. That is how we know it's working! We must measure the results. Not the effort. The results. This is one of those key things we must do to be successful, but please, in pursuit of data, don't measure things that don't matter. Over-measuring can create just as much of a burden as not measuring at all. And measuring effort is not the same as measuring results. Avoid this pitfalls when creating your metrics for success.

With that said, we must measure the results of our pilot project. As a rule of thumb, we should create measurements that complete the sentence: "How much of what by when."

For example:
"Increase number of customers serviced by 25 percent by the completion of the three-month pilot project."

"Decrease the time each citizen spends reporting issues by three minutes per transaction by April."

"Obtain 15 applicants for H.O.M.E. award by close of business on Friday."

There are many other books and websites we can read and reference on how to measure effectively, but I personally believe in using SMART or CLEAR goals with key performance measures tied to customer-focused outcomes, not outputs. It is not enough to measure how many potholes we fill, although that may be important to our management. But our customer, the resident, only cares about the time it takes to fill *their* pothole, so the most relevant measure is the time it takes to fill a pothole correctly once reported, not the total number of potholes filled.

Also, we need to do our best never to cheat the data—and to minimize others' ability to do so. Consider how automation of data collection might be possible. Measuring results is critical to your success and building *Sustainovation*. We can put the best foot forward in presenting results, but track honest and reliable data, and show it. Then be honest about results. It can be difficult to admit that a pilot project didn't create the results that we hoped for, but we need to remember that Thomas Edison failed over 1,000 times before he got the lightbulb to work, and it has gone through countless iterations after that. Being honest about what worked and what didn't enable us to determine what we need to fix to make it work; and it builds credibility in the future for new pilots.

Deal With The Outliers

When you get the data, look at those data points that are well outside the norm—the outliers. There is typically a relevant story in these data points. See if there are any common facts with these outliers that are good lessons for a future pilot, or that take your thoughts in a different direction. When looking at visualizations of data, we are looking for zebras, not horses. We are looking for things that stand out, not things that fit the narrative. Understand the outliers, why they occurred and what they might indicate.

And then throw these outliers out. Throw out any values that are too extreme and look at the data again. Outliers can influence an outcome by skewing averages and graphs in a way that prevents us from seeing real patterns. Remove outliers, visualize the data, and look for patterns and trends. Now what does the data tell us about the pilot project?

Blame-Free Autopsy

Regardless of whether we accomplish our goals or not, we hold a *Blame-Free Autopsy* on every pilot program. Spoiler alert: ideas don't work sometimes. We fail. Sometimes our ideas die horrible, tragic, spectacularly public deaths—and sometimes it's simply an accident. And sometimes we knock it out of the park, but best intentions do not always lead to the best ideas. Too often, on the back of a failed pilot project, the focus shifts quickly to "blamestorming" instead of learning what happened and seeing if it can be prevented or improved upon next time. If your organization is a bastion of blamestorming, you will stifle innovation, sow enmity among staff, and demoralize your brightest employees.

So we need to offer an alternative—every time—regardless of success or failure.

While the concept of a *Blame-Free Autopsy* may sound a bit grotesque, the idea is easy and not nearly as disturbing: Convene the entire team of people who worked on a given pilot project, determine the challenges and causes of failure and success without assigning blame or credit to people, and open lines of communication among the team. Talk about the contributing factors, processes, lessons learned, and impediments, but don't assign blame to specific people by name unless it cannot be avoided. If possible, do this no more than one week after the pilot project ends. This ensures the team still has it fresh in their heads.

The truth is, we must get into the nitty-gritty and disturbing truths about a project to learn from it. The better our team gets at separating the process and the outcome from the emotion and the blame, the better innovators we will create. The more *Sustainovation* we will build. Otherwise, our organization is one that talks about innovation but doesn't embrace one of its most fundamental tenets: *Our willingness to fail is intrinsically linked to our ability to succeed*. To succeed as an organization,

we need to pilot smart, pilot often, pilot fast and get honest about the results. This builds credibility with our audience when we have successful projects.

HERE ARE A FEW GUIDELINES FOR GOOD BLAME-FREE AUTOPSIES:

1. Start by convening all the players and setting the stage and expectations:
   a. "We will be doing a 'blame-free autopsy' today"
   b. Discussion should be honest
   c. Conversation should focus on being fact-based, not opinion-based
   d. Processes, not people, are the focus of the discussion
   e. The conversation can be heated but must be respectful
   f. The goal is to learn lessons for future innovations
2. The meeting should start with a discussion and recognition of what worked
3. Continue with a discussion on how the process worked and what didn't go as expected
4. The meeting should end with clear next steps, who is responsible, and when that is due

The regular, forensic, and fact-based examination of the project can be deeply uncomfortable for some people, but the honest examination allows the organization to become accustomed to the "right" innovation process, which includes learning from mistakes and embracing a culture that doesn't punish failure of this type. By sending a message that our organization will examine, but not punish, people for "failing," it encourages a culture of innovation, and employees will be more likely to come forward with ideas in the future.

So, if you work for an organization that is struggling with creating a culture of innovation, I encourage you to use the *"Blame-Free Autopsy"* to get the ball rolling, and hopefully you will find yourselves burying less failures and building more credibility.

Parting Thoughts...

By piloting smarter, learning about the languages and gray areas in your organization, keeping pilots short and small, creating a pipeline of ideas, and getting honest about the results, we can create credibility and space in the innovation equation. The more pilots we do, the more innovation space we create, and the more accepted it becomes. In fact, all this failing "the right way" will help you succeed faster the next time. And believe me, we will succeed *far* more than we will fail. In fact, you'll develop a reputation as someone who is moving the organization forward. You'll learn about how you operate best and learn about your organization's paradigm—making you even more successful.

TEAM US

Very few pilot projects and achievements in my career have come without an incredible team of people as part of them. I have been blessed to work alongside some very gifted and talented people in my career, and this was not an accident. My goal is to inspire people and help them find their passions, and that can build loyalty. I do my best to mentor and help support others growth and development. People ask me what I do for a living, and I tell them: I help great people do great things. It's true, and it's an approach I call *Team Us*. It's my leadership philosophy. It's part servant leadership, part *Drive-By Humanity*, part passion, and part inspiration.

Team Us is the key to a more collaborative world. It's about inviting people in instead of shutting them out. This is about the sum of us being stronger than the parts. It's about dialogue. It's about inspiring each other and being inspired. It's about finding a way to get to yes. It's about large-scale, drive-by humanity. This is the "future of the future" and what we need more of to make our communities great. It's a path that we can put ourselves on, but it's a journey we can take together. And it requires us to care about more than just ourselves.

Team Us is a philosophy rooted in servant leadership, but it also equal measure inspiration. It is about knowing our team and cultivating an environment where we value the contributions of everyone and set people up for success. Allow our team to work in their strengths and their passions—no matter where they are in the organization. *Team Us* is the right mindset for finding solutions and getting to yes. Find the people with the right attitude and abilities. Prioritize their projects and support their passions. We help them accomplish their goals, and we will get their help accomplishing ours. Create our coalition of the willing and able and build our *Team Us*. Think about who your "key players" are and start building your team. Have fun. Create a movement.

These are some guiding thoughts and *Team Us* principles to consider as you build out your team. *Team Us* is about achieving results *together*, so please note these are about building, growing, supporting and encouraging each other, but it is all in the service of a higher goal of achieving together, because a rising tide lifts all boats.

Find A Way To Get To Yes

This is a mentality that a mentor and former city manager of mine used all the time. She really beat it into my head, and she was right. It's the right mental state to begin. When working on major projects with large obstacles or when working with difficult groups, it helps to say this at the start of a meeting. It is a powerful phrase: "My goal today is to find a way to get to yes. I'm hoping you can help me." This does not mean getting everything you wanted, but it is a mindset for looking for solutions, not problems. We can use it to encourage people back on course when things get challenging and people get off focus. We can use it to prevent anyone from feeling alienated by making them a part of the larger team. Finding a way to get to yes is about finding possibility, not pitfalls. Encourage the group to develop the path to make an idea work, to learn how we get flexible, and to realize where we can't. Identify win-win and good compromise opportunities. I find this tool to be particularly useful when I'm working with lawyers or risk personnel in a contentious organization. It's an invitation to be part of the solution.

Mirthwhile

If you're not having fun, you're doing it wrong! Make your effort "mirthwhile": making something worthwhile because you're having fun (yes, this is a *Sniglet*). When building momentum, having fun can be a key aphrodisiac to growing your team and their commitment to the cause. If you have a choice between two projects, and one is fun and the other is not, which one would you choose?

Having fun certainly doesn't hurt. Keep the meetings short and moving. Joke around. Hold meetings outdoors. Bring snacks. Take walks. Include whimsical events and celebrate people's wins together. Keep it fun. Make it *mirthwhile*. Then get the work done and crush it. Have fun, but make sure you're being focused on moving the needle while you do it. The truth is, if you're having fun and getting results, people will want to keep working on your team. Never leave your longings unattended.

Give Credit

We need to recognize that there are two types of credit for success with a project: idea generation credit, which recognizes the people who create an idea, and implementation credit, which recognizes those who made it happen. Both are critical roles in innovation, but rarely do we focus on giving *both* types credit. This leads to resentment by either the people who came up with the idea or by those who did the work. By remembering to give both types credit, we are ensuring we recognize all the project collaborators.

To help give out idea generation credit, ask yourself who was the person or team responsible for generating the idea. Many times, the person or people generating

the idea are different than the team that has to implement the idea, so be sure to recognize those that helped create the idea.

To find who should receive implementation credit, answer the question "Who was the person or team responsible for implementing the idea?" Few ideas would become an innovation without a team of great people implementing them, so be sure to call out implementers and recognize these team members as well.

A good example of the need for both is penicillin. Penicillin has saved between 80 and 200 million people since its discovery. Alexander Fleming is credited with its discovery, but he could not isolate its active compounds, meaning he could not commercialize it or keep it alive long enough to be used for medical purposes. Enter Australian Howard Florey and German refugee Ernst Chain, who began working with penicillin and could isolate, replicate, and commercialize it for use. Without the discovery by Fleming, Florey and Chain would have had nothing to develop, and without Florey and Chain, the marvel of Fleming's discovery would have gone unrealized.

It is important for an innovation leader to recognize the need to give credit to both parties. As we develop our innovation skills, it is important that we work to get comfortable giving credit to others for magnificent work, which encourages more collaboration and success. If there is the perception of a failure, it is our job to acknowledge it, own it, and step in on behalf of the team. Our job is to *give* credit; we *take* blame. This helps us build loyal teams who are happy, if not eager, to collaborate with us in the future. As much as possible, talk about the team who made it happen. This requires discipline in knowing you might not personally get "credit" right away, but great innovation is its own reward, and giving credit to others will pay dividends in the long run.

Celebrate Wins

And when we succeed, as we certainly will—when we score that ever-sweet victory of implementing our creative idea or helping someone else get theirs implemented— *celebrate*. If you have an awards or incentive program, nominate someone on the team for an award. Celebrating as a team solidifies the win and motivates the team to do more clever work. Eat an ice cream cake or go to a park and play volleyball. Take time out of life to celebrate the wins, because that's what makes the innovation risk worth it. Invite the idea generators and idea implementers. Give credit. Thank people for their roles in making it a success. And take time to just savor the win and celebrate with your team!

Support Other's Passions

One of the most effective ways to build our *Team Us* is to help others find what they are passionate about and support their passions. Continuing to help others find and build on their passions will let you shine by helping others shine. When founding our city's sustainability efforts, we used personal passions to move the cause forward and grow a movement. It's how we built momentum and grew a coalition. For example, we learned about the passions and strengths of our team, and when faced with a task of starting a recycling program for city facilities and had zero funds to get it done, we partnered with a local recycling company to procure "fiber-barrel" bins for nearly free and partnered with local artists and employees to decorate them. To make it fun, the bins were "judged" by local media celebrities, garnering media attention, and the bins were placed throughout city facilities with the names of the local artists who decorated them. We leveraged the passion and the talents of our local businesses, our local artists, our employees, and our citizens to drive the project to success.

Which brings me back to passion. The best kind of support you can give and get is from a place of passion. By learning about people's passions, we can look for opportunities to marry passion with opportunity. Often, I will ask someone I am just meeting "what are you passionate about?" It is surprising the fascinating variety of conversations you will have from there. Make it a habit to learn about people's passions when getting to know them, and if you can, help them take a step towards working in that passion. So many times in my career, I have helped someone take a step in the direction of doing what they are passionate about, and those are some of my most rewarding moments. It is amazing to me how few people actively pursue what they are passionate about as part of their work, but it is a great driver for success. And most importantly, the impact on someone when you help them find their way toward their passion is staggering. As you might imagine, many of these people are now my friends and have helped me on a variety of pilot projects in return. This conscious effort to help people work within their passions is a huge part of building momentum, and a big part of the philosophy of *Team Us*.

"I Believe" Statements

Talking about what you believe can be an important part of getting others to buy in. This is about getting to know your team and letting them get to know you. Develop a personal manifesto or even a team vision that people can get behind. Simply start with "I believe," and keep writing. Tap into your inner beliefs and speak. Keep it short and powerful – a message of hope, aspiration, possibility, inspiration or strength. If you're writing it for an organization, start with "We believe" and go from there. Here are a couple of personal examples, and you can see that while both are true, they speak to different audiences entirely—but you learn more about me from reading them. What is your "I Believe" statement?

"I believe innovation is creativity implemented. Innovation requires us to become stronger at changing our perspective, selecting a great idea, building support, selling it, and making it happen. I believe innovation starts with one person and can grow into a movement and a culture."

"I believe great and sustained innovation in government requires pro-social Machiavellianism and a passion for disrupting comfort. I believe complacency and apathy are the enemy of great innovation."

Know Your Strengths

We must know our strengths—and those of our team. Using our strengths allows us to focus on areas where we excel and build teams with complementary skill sets, allowing everyone to focus on where they are strong. But first we must know what those skill sets and strengths are. Using Clifton StrengthsFinder to identify your areas of strength is a terrific way to explore and develop your skills, and I'm personally an enthusiastic fan; however, there are many personality assessment or leadership language tools you can use. Pick the one that's right for you and figure out what your team is strong at.

What I like about the Clifton StrengthsFinder framework is that it allows us to work on those skills that we are inherently pre-disposed to be good at. By exercising our strengths and minimizing our weaknesses, and asking our team to do the same, we can remain engaged, excited, and strong. We can then find others with complimentary skills to round out our teams, allowing each of us to work in areas where we have comparatively more talent and desire. Determine an assessment tool that your team is comfortable with and have them take it—use it as a common language among the team. Spend time discussing how to build pilot projects that use everyone's best skills. By using people's strengths and their passions, we are setting up *Team Us* for success.

Oh, and once you have an inventory of your skills, remember to develop them! Find ways to practice developing your skills so you can become more adept. The more we build teams around strengths and passion, the less we have to work in a space that we don't like.

Be Persistent; Get Determined

This is about continuing to push forward in the face of obstacles. I tried five times to build a disc golf course before I was successful. It took me six years to get it done. I didn't let the first four failures deter me; I got persistent. I got determined. When a project looks impossible is when a normal person would stop. That cannot be us. We must continue to persist and push forward. In government, it is often a game of caring and continuing to push, very slowly but very constantly. Steady and forward. You should be persistent and get determined. Encourage this in your team. Support them when it seems difficult and when your team gets discouraged. Face the facts head on, have a freak-out moment, suck it up, and get back to work. I promise you will feel all the stronger when you do accomplish goals with your team, knowing you did it together through adversity.

Build Momentum

Once you have your *Team Us* assembled, it's time to start building momentum. As anyone who has ever played organized sports or anyone who is the least bit competitive can tell you, momentum is a critical element of winning. There are key moments in games where the momentum shifts in one team's favor or another, and these shifts can lead to victory. Innovation is like that as well. When you're feeling creative, ride that wave for as long as it lasts – sometimes minutes, sometimes days. When you're starting a project, find the things you can "just do," and get the small wins started.

And small wins lead to bigger wins. When starting off with implementation, it's important for the team to start getting wins quickly. Many big projects require months and years of challenging work to accomplish. Getting small wins quickly demonstrates momentum on a project, and it's critical to success. Let's face it: People like to be on winning teams, and there is nothing like getting a few small wins under your belt early on to get the team focused on the longer road to bigger wins.

We built a successful sustainability movement in a conservative community from the ground-up, by using momentum. Our first meeting had eight attendees; our next had

16 and then 32. We asked for each person to bring just one more person who was as passionate as they were. We grew smarter and got engaged and invited people to be a part. We focused our initial efforts on "just do its" that required very few resources to get started: bike tours, education events, grant applications, a green fair, etc., and moved our way into recycling programs and building retrofits. These efforts ultimately allowed us to build and prove the value of a four million-dollar office in less than three years, using only ten thousand dollars in seed money. Momentum is all about small wins turning into bigger wins.

Lead. Whether They Want You To Or Not.

When innovating, many times it is necessary to lead a team, a coalition, a program, or a project, whether we want to or not. True leadership is not something you get permission to do. It is something you just do. And sometimes you have to do it whether you want to or not. Innovation is a space where people do not always understand what you are doing, and that's okay. *We* have the vision of how it is possible, how it will work, how it could be great, not them. That is why we must lead whether others want us to or not. Which means people will not always want you to succeed. I find that people in government are wired to slow down innovation if they don't get it—and sometimes even when they do. Get persistent. Use your team. Find a way to get to yes. But move forward.

And when you believe in an idea, and people just don't get it, you need to ask forgiveness, not permission. This is not something others will likely tell you, but I can't stress enough how much we need to quit apologizing for doing our jobs before we even start. We were hired to do a job. Do it. Of course, there are consequences for trying something new, but consequences can be good and bad. If we believe in an idea, we must be willing to accept the consequences of implementing it. But I've found that many times in innovating, acceptance happens only *after an idea works*. And if it doesn't, there will be plenty of people who get to say, "I told you so" and silently marvel at your courage to try and "fail." When you succeed, your detractors may or may not get more silent, but you will find more supporters and create a louder voice—an army of "can do" to offset and overwhelm any negative voice. It is amazing how that works. With a few small wins, you will find more and more people getting on board *before*. And for those that don't get on board, do your best to bring them along, but keep going.

We must trust our vision, trust our idea, and just start doing it. This means asking for forgiveness sometimes. But that's okay and part of the journey to becoming a better innovator. I'll say it again: our willingness to fail is directly linked to how much we succeed with innovation. And when you ask for forgiveness or get beaten up for an idea that didn't work like you hoped, *learn the lesson* so you don't make the same mistake again.

While we always hope to have universal support for an idea and our path to innovation, the truth is that is not what happens. The truth is, not asking people for permission will ruffle some feathers, but that's okay. People will oppose you at different points if you are innovating hard enough. The car was resisted. Factory automation was resisted. Every truly disruptive idea has been. People fear change, and we need to consider whether we want to fear change as well. If not, we cannot allow people to stand in our way. The mission of government innovation is too important. There is a cost to doing nothing and innovation requires us to have the courage of our convictions.

So lead. Whether they want you to or not.

Parting Thoughts...

Team Us is my leadership philosophy on how to build supportive innovation teams. We need the help of others to achieve amazing innovation, especially in hard-to-move systems like government. These principles are part of building a team of talented people that are committed to achieving, celebrating and innovating together. If we approach people with the right attitude, passion and enthusiasm we can create an environment where people feel supported to achieve. We can celebrate the wins, give credit and help each other find our passions. We can do all this and achieve amazing results. That is how *Team Us* works.

ACTIONISMS

In my experience, taking the first step can be one of the most difficult parts of the journey of innovation. Trying something out takes a lot of courage, the courage of a *Map Maker*, and many times a "good enough" plan is delayed in search of a perfect plan. We see this all the time in the hallowed halls of government—plans sitting on shelves collecting dust. There are a variety of tools or techniques you can use to get off the starting line with your idea, and that's what this section is about. Actionisms are a collection of thoughts and concepts around how to help get ideas off the ground. This is part of the philosophy about how to approach innovation. Again, not every idea is needed for every situation, but hopefully these will help you take action on your pilot projects.

"People without vision should never tell people with vision what to do."
- Nick Kittle

Doing Nothing Has Consequences

When establishing the urgency of a situation or encouraging action, it is necessary to talk about the consequences of doing nothing. Yes, doing nothing has a consequence. Continuing to underfund fleet replacement, or to defer bridge maintenance, or to not increase pay of your employees has consequences. Some are short term, and some are long term. But there are consequences. It is important for you to discuss and write down the possible impacts of what happens if we do nothing, so you can prepare the full picture and describe it.

Think about how different the world would be if we talked as much about what happens *if we do nothing* as we do about dealing with the fear of change. Doing nothing creates scary consequences for many things, so talking about the "do nothing" consequence can make "change" less scary.

Spend time practicing thinking about what happens in the future if we do nothing. If there is no major consequence for doing nothing, then you likely do not have a *compelling why* and will have a tough time getting people on board with the idea.

Establish Urgency

Implementing innovation is much easier when there is a sense of urgency. A compelling why. A push to get it done now.

When facing a $27 million budget shortfall, Colorado Springs invited all its employees to town hall meetings, where facilitated brainstorming was used to identify processes and practices that were outdated and could be changed to save the city money. The employees knew that layoffs, furloughs, and wage cuts were almost certain, so there was an urgent motivation to put the best ideas out there. Out of 880 different ideas that came forth over three days, 12 of them were developed further and implemented, and these ideas collectively cut $12 million of the shortfall. Think about that: When it came to the direst situation employees could conceive, they closed nearly 50 percent of the budgetary gap through collaboration and ideation. Many of these eliminated or transformed practices that had been in place for years, and some of the ideas, such as having the fire department train in specific parks so the water would fall on the underwatered grass, were wild and different. And it was easy to get people on board to implement most of these ideas because they recognized the imminent threat posed by the budgetary shortfall.

It was the urgency that created freedom for ideas, some wild and some previously rejected, to gain support and create an easy path to implementation. The urgency of needing to do it *right now* compelled both ideas and action.

In his famous TED talk, Simon Sinek talks about the need for a *compelling why*. "People don't buy what you do, they buy why you do it," says Sinek. This is true for effective implementation. If people understand and are connected to *why* you are doing something, they will work with blood, sweat, and tears. The compelling *why* is an emotional connection. People in Colorado Springs weren't connected to the concept of a $27 million shortfall—that was urgency. People were connected to the emotional connection of having a job—or not having a job. That was the *compelling why*. If you can't articulate why implementing your innovation should happen *right now*, people will simply not be as engaged, leading to a lack of enthusiasm and limiting your support. Use crisis and urgency to spur action.

Make A Decision

The truth is, in many cases it is hard to know which answers are "right" and which ones are "wrong" in taking a step forward. Far too many great projects don't get off the ground because people are unwilling or unable to make a decision. Many times, those tasked with making the decision, such as executives and directors, are not as well informed as the people who will *bypass* the option of making decisions in the creative process. Having high-level buy-in during the implementation phase is important, but decision-making in the creative phase should come from those most invested in the idea—and that can be anyone.

This is an important concept in the creative space as well as in the implementation space. In the process of being creative, we are faced with many variables and unknowns. In those moments, we should weigh out the options and decide. There is a risk and fear with decision-making that the decision will turn out to be the wrong one. If information that is contrary comes to light later in the process, we need to be fluid and adapt our concept to meet these facts, but in the absence of knowledge about the outcomes, we should make decisions based on the best information available. For ideas to become real, we must make decisions, sometimes hard ones, but 100 percent of the projects that never took the first step failed.

Eating The Elephant

This powerful metaphor and real-world example from nature is a disgusting guidepost on the truth of where to begin when dealing with changing any large, monolithic system like government, and it's all about taking a step forward any way you can. We've all heard the adage: "How do you eat an elephant? One bite at a time."

The metaphor is designed to teach the lesson of getting started and realizing it's going to take a while. But let's get disgustingly literal: Do you know how an elephant really gets eaten? Yes, it is one bite at a time—at first—then it is many bites at a time. So what about that first impossible bite?

The first bite isn't by the top predators, but by the jackal or hyena. And where do you think the hyena *enters* the elephant to take the first bite? That's right, the nastiest way you can imagine. The first bite of the elephant often happens in the most disgusting and accessible part of the elephant—the ass. And that nose-deaf courage to take the first bite is rewarded with a full belly, which is akin to life in the African prairies. And while that stomach-turning mental imagery might be distressing you mightily right now (hopefully you aren't eating), look past the literal story, and you will see a valuable lesson on making massive changes to large, slow, bureaucratic systems.

The best way to take a first bite and begin to tackle the change required for any government-like system is to go right for the most disgusting and accessible part of the system. What is the thing that no one else wants to touch or tackle? Start there. What part of the system makes the greatest stink for the customers or the least pleasant interaction point? Start there. What is the part that allows you the easiest access to more opportunities for change? That is where you should start. The first bite creates momentum for the team and the right first bite allows others access as well. Even if it smells to high heaven. Be nose-deaf.

Speaking of smelling, a decade ago, a city manager I worked for asked for a volunteer to "start" the city's sustainability efforts. So we did. The city had been engaging in environmental efforts, but they were department-led and poorly tracked, and there were few coordinated efforts. The community felt it had no support to protect the environment. But as anyone familiar with the field knows, "sustainability" is an elephant. With a recycling rate that was one-third the national average, the community sustainability team that came together decided to target waste/recycling as their priority.

And so, when we took up the challenge, we started in the smelliest and most accessible place: waste. At the time, our community had limited access to cardboard, glass, and plastics recycling. There were very few incentives to engage in conservation behaviors because of a local recycling monopoly, so we created the incentives and eliminated barriers. At the same time, we held a meeting that put the five largest private haulers (over 85 percent of the local market) on notice that recycling was going to be a mandatory part of the future—and would soon be required of all of them. At first their tough exterior was resistant to change. They were shocked, and one of their reps stormed out of the room after threatening my job. As the designated spokesperson, I bluffed hard and took a calculated risk. We didn't have the votes to force a mandate, but when the situation changed, we knew the resistance would be picked clean away. We took the first bite.

One day later, one of the five biggest haulers decided to start single-stream recycling and expand their offerings to include glass, plastics #3-7 and residential cardboard. The rep for one hauler said that they'd known it was coming and needed us to push the status quo to make it possible. Then another of the haulers came forward. And another. All of them were on board by the end of that same month, and within a year, the diversion rate for the community had more than doubled.

Taking the metaphor one step further, eating the elephant returns incredibly valuable nutrients to the organizational ecosystem, just like in tackling a bureaucracy. The largest elephants are holding on to the most resources of your organization, and by tackling these large elephants, we will release massive amounts of energy back into the organization. Think about your projects and where your organization spends its effort. Think about the largest systems that produce the least value and the amount of resources it can take to prop them up. If you can eat the elephant, there is a massive amount of capital returned to the organization. And government is always able to redeploy its resources.

The last key in this stomach-churning metaphor is that the hyena, even though it takes the first bite, doesn't eat the elephant alone. Once the process begins, other large scavengers and predators begin to help; everyone is doing its part in the process, all the way down to the birds and insects cleaning the bones at the end. This is also akin to how we need to work collectively to tackle huge system changes. It requires not just one, but several key team members, to provide momentum, and then many other players swarming on the problem to get any massive change completed. In essence, the person who takes the first bold bite should not be required to carry the project through to completion. It is not their burden alone, and any momentous change should involve a series of players equipped to handle their part.

I share the rest of the tale in hopes that the metaphor will live on in a new way, renewed in its meaning for those of you who are bold *Map Makers*, or for those of you tackling huge changes. While I didn't necessarily want to insert an image in your head that you won't shake, the full story completes an age-old lesson for us all. Cheers to your elephant. Let's eat.

Ready. Fire. Aim.

Ready. Fire. Aim. And then shoot. You may not hit the bullseye, but you will hit the target. Trust your abilities. Take another step on the project and then another. Correct your aim on your next shot, and shoot again. And again, and again. You miss 100 percent of the shots you don't take.

Just as when you shoot an arrow at a target as a novice, your hand will likely be unsteady, and "hidden factors" such as wind will remain unimportant because you have so little real skill. As you shoot and become more adept at shooting, you start to factor in for these "hidden elements" that might influence the accuracy of your shot. Eventually, with enough practice, you're able to make these calculations on the fly and shoot an accurate arrow the first time. But it happens with practice. And that means you must fire and take a shot. Olympic archers learned by shooting arrows, not planning on shooting arrows.

This can be the hardest part. Sometimes it is just taking one step forward, and then we find the brilliance comes. Many times, the paralysis comes from analysis. From an abundance of caution. From the desire to perfect the idea. To strategize it until it is flawless and accounts for every contingency. To avoid any consequences.

The truth is, projects are dynamic, and while it is important to develop a solid strategy for implementing a great idea, it is just as important to get started. Momentum is big in innovation.

Consent Vs Consensus

This mistake happens on many government projects. People conflate consent and consensus. Too many times we shoot for consensus instead of what we really need: consent. This can hold us back from acting, so be sure to carefully consider which of these you really need. If people have authority over key areas where you need partnership, be sure to gain their buy-in and support. But if someone does not have the authority to stop the project, we do not need to ask their permission, so we are looking for consent. Consensus is about everyone agreeing, and that is very hard to do. It can take a very long time in many cases—especially things that could be potentially polarizing like a disruptive innovation. This means most of the time we really want consent, which is a lesser bar to clear. Do not give away authority unnecessarily, and don't require consensus when all you need is consent.

Make Your Own Luck

One way to increase your chances of hitting the target right out of the gate is to think about as many possible outcomes as possible and prepare for as many of those as you can. Luck and chance favor a prepared mind. Sometimes luck is about being prepared to react to all eventualities. Sometimes it is about the attitude with which you approach it. Henry Ford said, "Whether you think you can, or think you can't, you're right." Luck is a function of preparation and belief—and so much beyond our control. To increase our chances of success, we can strategize and prepare ourselves for the most likely outcomes.

Flip It

In my experience, people have a tough time seeing past what is right in front of them. They have a tough time seeing the inherent opportunity just beyond the gray. For example, we had an old fleet in Colorado Springs; meaning our fleet was worth less if there was an issue with our biodiesel experiments. Budgets were always getting tighter, and there was no money for office supplies, which meant office supplies were in high demand, and reusing them was an opportunity that would get interest. If no one oversees something, become in charge of it yourself. When morale is low, it means there is an opportunity for someone to lead and inspire. Not having enough people to get the job done means more flexibility and less oversight. If there is a community crisis, it means people are paying attention. Beware that the opposite is also true: If you're well-funded and well-staffed, there is no less incentive to change and more protections for "ok is good enough," unless you find and establish urgency. You can see how each of these examples is mostly about how you look at it. So, whatever your disadvantage is, flip your thinking, and turn it into your advantage.

Change Incentives, Change Behavior

So many times, we find the incentives or disincentives in an organization are the real reason people engage in the behavior they do. When considering your organization's readiness for innovation, consider the incentives that are in place. Do they support innovation or keeping the status quo? What incentives are in place for those who innovate? Are your pay practices, awards programs, or reward structures geared towards those who "toe the line" or towards those who take risks? There are countless examples where incentives hold us back or prevent us from encouraging organizational creativity.

When considering the incentives we put in place, it is important to consider what behaviors they might unintentionally create. If a city measures the number of potholes filled, the goal becomes to fill more potholes. But that might encourage staff to change the definition of a pothole to increase the number or to reduce the quality of the repair to fit more repairs in. What happens if you fill more potholes, but they don't last as long? Have we incentivized the right behavior? Take the time to consider the organizational incentives that might influence your success.

Add Competition And Gamify

Whenever possible, we should add competition to our pilot projects and use people's natural competitive drive to move the needle on our innovation. In addition, the more we can make that competition like a game and build on the principle of having fun, the more we design systems built for results. Competition has been used to drive performance since mankind evolved. For example, we were trying to demonstrate widespread community support for sustainability projects and kept encountering the false perception that there wasn't as much support as there was. To combat that perception and demonstrate how easy sustainable choices can be, we developed an Earth Month contest that encouraged people to do up to 20 simple, sustainable activities and take pictures of themselves while doing them. Each activity was a ticket in the grand prize drawing ($300). We found business sponsors for several of the sustainability photo categories ("Best Alternative Commuting Photo," etc.), created a Facebook page, and posted the competition. We had expected a few hundred photos in our first year and were surprised with well over a thousand photo entries! At the end of the contest, we selected the winners and gave away a total of

$600 in donated prizes. We now had thousands of photos demonstrating community support, as well as an actual community supporting our projects, which allowed us to make a much larger, successful funding request. Not necessarily earth-shattering (no pun intended), but certainly a fantastic way to use natural human tendency to our advantage and get action behind our idea. And remember, some people are motivated by individual challenges and some are motivated by team challenges, so be sure to choose the right type of competition to get your effort going.

So, as we put action behind our ideas, consider how to add in game elements to increase participation and drive results. And when you get the competition going, heat things up and talk a little trash from time to time! Just have some fun—and kick some ass.

Parting Thoughts...

Actionisms are about getting off the line and are a collection of helpful thoughts, analogies, metaphors and invocations that will hopefully set your mind in the right place to begin acting on your innovation. Understanding and articulating the urgency, making decisions, and turning our disadvantages around are just a few of the great ways we can get off the starting line and take a first step with our innovative idea!

BUILD YOUR ARMOR

This is the part of innovation where I talk tough to you. The part where I help you understand what it truly takes to do this well. More than one great aspiring innovator I know has been sidelined by an inability to grow thicker skin. Part of getting good at innovation is learning to build up your personal armor. Look, it's going to be tough at times, so it's important to learn how to be mentally resilient when facing resistance or withering criticism when things don't go as planned. This is not a psychology book (well maybe a little), and I don't have a degree, but in doing over 65 pilot projects, I have taken it on the chin more than a few times while implementing ideas. Here are a few thoughts designed to help you get your head in the right place and some techniques to thicken up your armor when you encounter people who are against your idea or you're encountering resistance.

Lose The Fear of Failure

Yes, easier said than done. But hear me out: This *one thing* may make your life great.

Great organizations and communities do this. They try ideas. They fail. They iterate. They try again. That's why it is so important to lose the fear of failure. Failure and success are intrinsically linked. If you fear failing, you will have a challenging time truly innovating. If you're afraid of looking foolish, you can't truly innovate. You must lose the fear of failure. It's a key ingredient because the bigger the failures you can stomach, the bigger successes you can gain.

So many times, I've stood in front of people and had to look like a fool to move an idea forward. And I've failed in some spectacular ways on my way to some very large successes.

One example was when I was locking fuel prices for Colorado Springs. I had been successful in "beating the market" four years in a row, even though that was never the goal. The goal was to use fuel hedges to stabilize fuel prices for budgetary purposes. Being "right" and "beating the market" had increased the pressure, and inevitably, the global economic collapse in 2008 sent fuel prices plummeting. Our "locks" on fuel prices were much higher than the market, meaning we were losing about $2 million in unnecessary fuel costs. As you can imagine, people freaked out, and when things turned darkest, my job was in jeopardy. I remember being yelled at by an assistant city manager after the local newspaper suggested I was recklessly gambling with taxpayer dollars. People who previously lauded my ability to lock pricing were suddenly critics of the "insane" risks I was taking—*even though they had agreed with the decision at the time.* The goal was always to stabilize the fuel costs to improve our ability to budget and plan and hedge our risk, and I was very clear about that—but I was a victim of my own success. I had four years of locking prices with some very positive consequences. I had even warned this might happen. And I soon learned an important lesson: 4-out-of-5 was the same as 0-for-1. But instead of giving up, I doubled-down. It took a once-in-a-lifetime global recession to make the ever-rising fuel market plummet, and that created new opportunity. I created a partnership with our local utility (who used our fuel as well) and found a place to store the higher-priced fuel for a two-year period, providing a source of valuable emergency fuel, and then re-locked the fuel at new market-low prices. By the time the two years had expired, the fuel prices had rebounded, and we had turned a $2 million loss into a $1.5 million gain.

Never Be Afraid to Get Fired

But this leads to another crucial point about being effective: Never be afraid to get fired. Through the years, I have met many CEOs and have asked them all one question: "What is the one piece of advice you would give to someone who wants to be a leader?" Invariably, they all answer with some version of "never be afraid to get fired." Most of them have been fired from multiple jobs and continue to land new jobs because they trust their skills. They try, and experiment, and make tough decisions, and learn. Sometimes they get fired. And no matter what, they get better at it and keep going and growing. It is certainly true for me.

While I'm not suggesting you should *strive* to get fired, there is a boldness required to be a successful innovator, and there is a possibility that others will not understand or will never get on board. Just don't fear being fired. If you're good, you will land on your feet.

Build Pockets of Positivity

To turn around a stagnant culture and encourage an environment for innovation, one that is geared towards action, we can cultivate *Pockets of Positivity* (POP).

These are safe places of positivity, experimentation, and support, where people can give themselves permission to be happy and excited and feel like it's cool to achieve results, like it's cool to care. It is the general nature of humans in large groups to talk more about the negative than the positive. But this kind of mindset is counterproductive to innovation. A culture of "no" and "blame" creates an environment where innovation fails. To succeed, we need to start carving out safe places for innovation to happen.

To do this, we must surround ourselves with people whom we admire for their "can-do" and positive attitude. Form a secret society if you must. To build your own POP, just find the five people you know who are a joy to be around. Ask them whether they are tired of the griping and complaining. Ask if they would be your teammates in giving each other *permission* to be positive. Ask if they would join your *Pocket of Positivity*. All that means is that you will greet each other, support each other, tell the positive tales of life, and generally try to enjoy the work environment, etc. In short, you will give each other permission and support to be happy at work and be excited for each other's successes. This is not a place to complain about work or to engage in gossip. It's a safe space—a *Pocket of Positivity*.

Obliterate Energy Vampires

Let me introduce you to our enemy: the energy vampires. The energy vampires have many faces, but they have one common purpose: to suck our positive energy, to make us feel less than whole. If you're happy, they want to stamp it out. They have many tools and guises at their disposal: drama, doubt, one-upmanship, passive-aggressiveness, aggressiveness, uncertainty, control, insincerity. The list goes on. But they all want the same thing: for us to quit being so positive about our life.

Don't you realize how bad it all is? Don't you know that it may be okay now but that you're just a stone's throw away from utter disaster? Don't you know what management is really doing behind closed doors? Don't you know that Martha told John that she didn't really like your outfit? Don't you know? Ugh. Over it.

In our personal lives, we can avoid these dramatic demons more easily, and if we don't, that's our choice, but in the workplace, we are forced to interact with those who might try to take our happiness from us. Don't let them. Fight back. Assault them with positivity. High-five them when they aren't ready for it. Kill them with kindness. Call them out publicly if need be. To build an innovation culture, we are in a fight for the soul of the middle 80 percent of employees and they need to see that it's safe to care and cool to achieve. Because it is.

Consider The Source

One technique I use is to care less about other people's opinions is to "consider the source." Who is the source of the opinion and do you want to be like this person? If yes, then heed their advice, but still make up your own mind. But if you *don't* want to be like this person, then you don't have to bother caring what they think about you. Truly. It's not that you don't *want* to, but you don't *need* to, and that is usually enough to allow me to move past criticisms that are more personal than professional. This is easier said than done, but once you practice it, it becomes easier, and it makes it much faster to make progress on your innovations in the face of criticism. If you don't aspire to be like them, then why do you care what they think of you? Always consider the source.

I had one co-worker in particular with whom I did not get along. He was the kind of individual who would always work behind your back because he was suffering from a debilitating case of *GOWG Syndrome* (the need for control with no vision to make it happen). He was in a powerful position in the organization and would mutter aspersions about me and generally sow enmity and discord among the employees. He was very political and undermined me to anyone who would listen (as he did to many others). The truth was he was not very good at his job, and I had been improving activities in his work team, which was threatening to him no matter how I approached him. I actively confronted him to let him know he needed to wash my name out of his mouth, which shocked him. He was an energy vampire, and I called him out. It was direct, not rude. He redoubled his efforts of backbiting over the next few weeks, and as people got to know more about me and more about his true character, it became a badge of honor. "The source" was well recognized as someone whom people did not respect, so their attempts to disrupt my efforts became hollow and transparent. Just because someone criticizes you, don't always take the bait. The lion doesn't care about the opinion of sheep. Consider the source.

Watch The Movie

When things get contentious and people get rough, as they sometimes will, I use a technique where I try to write the story of the "movie in my mind" that I'm seeing. I write it in my head from the point of view of a third party, looking at the scene as if it were in a movie or book:

"Ben crossed the room looking dull in his tan suit but seeming ready to brawl. As he opened his mouth, it was obvious that this was going to be a yelling meeting. And as sure as it was obvious, he opened his mouth, and the fury of his roar came pelting towards me, stinging those as it passed until it landed in my lap for consideration. Sure, the process hadn't worked like we had intended, but suffering this guy every time was becoming almost pageant-like in its pomp and circumstance."

As you can see, it's just about describing the scene and the people in it. It allows me to detach myself from the events unfolding around me that might otherwise be quite stressful, maintain a positive demeanor, and focus on what's truly important. Even stressful, hard, awkward, and painful moments are sometimes funny—when they are happening to someone else on TV or in a movie. If the story wasn't happening to you, would it be funny at all? Could you re-write it in your head to fit a sitcom? What can you do to detach from the emotion being directed at you and continue to be true to the goal?

Forgive Yourself—and Others

It can be difficult after a project doesn't perform as well as we would like to resist the urge to beat ourselves up—or to do it to others. To engage in negative self-talk about what you "should have known" or what you would have done differently. Guess what? That's in the past. The only way to get where you want to go is to learn from the mistakes, make improvements to the idea, or process and try again. To get back up and try again is the fastest way to succeed. This requires forgiving ourselves—and others—for making mistakes and is an important part of being able to "shake off failure" and return to productive innovation. We all make mistakes, but it's how we recover that counts.

People Get On Board After

The truth is that sometimes people can't see what we see. The *River of our Experience* is different for every person, so we don't perceive the world in the same way. Sometimes people don't or won't understand your vision. Sometimes they just disagree.

But if we believe in an idea, and we believe it can do something great, we should invest despite those that don't get on board. To truly influence change and make larger innovations, we must understand that there will be resistance at some point or on some level. If we believe in the idea and we can proceed, do so anyway. Track our results. Learn lessons. Iterate. Try again.

And we will find over time that those who said no and those who doubted us may grow even more resentful of our ability to innovate—or they will find themselves rooting the loudest about our project's success. They may even talk about their role in the project. It's not unusual for people to gravitate towards the spotlight of success when a particularly excellent idea comes to life. If you want to encourage their support next time, give them a little breathing room, but don't let them take credit from the people who rightfully deserve it. Giving credit is an important part of an innovation culture, but just know people might jump on the bandwagon. Welcome them. The more the merrier.

GOWG Syndrome

I'm a big believe that people without vision should never tell people with vision what to do. *Grumpy Old White Guy* (GOWG) *Syndrome* is the need for control without the vision to back it up. *GOWG Syndrome* is NOT limited to old white guys, nor are all old white guys affected. It is a mentality that I tend to see most in grumpy old white guys. These people come off as serious people who are required for any decision. If they can't see how to do it, they also can't see how you could do it either. People afflicted with this syndrome believe they must be in control—but can't deliver on a vision when they are. This can affect anyone, but I've seen it in more grumpy, old white guys because they are predominately at the top of most local governments and in many cases enamored with their fiefdom.

These people rising to the tops of our organization is a serious flaw in our human dynamic. Many times, there are people who will decide that an innovation is frivolous, or they will decide that the only way to sell the idea is to make sure they agree first. They often exist in authority roles, and that is unfortunate, but I would encourage you not to defer to "serious people" just because they assume a demeanor appropriate for a funeral parlor and expect you to as well. Innovation is fun, and it is okay to be excited about an idea and run with it. If you believe in what you are doing, don't let this kind of personality overwhelm or overpower you. Don't allow someone afflicted with *GOWG Syndrome* to take your idea away or kill your passion. Not everyone is going to get it, and "no" people don't deserve the right. They may hate it, but you don't have to.

Toward the end of my tenure in Colorado Springs, I heard a story about Tahama Springs, the original spring of Colorado Springs that was destroyed in 1935 and again in 1965 by severe flooding. As a private citizen, I started investigating whether the spring was still there. I found a group who has been working on the spring and knew its history, so I sat down with them to learn more. What I quickly found was that this group liked the idea of the spring but had not taken any real action on it in over a decade. They were "squatting" on the project, and with one or two exceptions, the group was infected with *GOWG Syndrome*. I asked whether the spring was still active and was told they had *looked* down the hole, and it looked dry. But that was not the kind of thing you could tell by looking. They hadn't done any testing and were content to talk about it as an abstraction rather than as an opportunity to rally the community. They were very curious as to why I was asking questions about "their spring."

I asked them whether they would support us doing official testing, and they said they would, but they "knew" I wouldn't find anything. We did find something—the spring was still active. It just needs to be repaired. A new structure needs to be built. A great community architect had already designed the structure based on the original plans and put his work behind it pro bono—so we knew we were looking at roughly $350,000 to get it constructed.

I reached out to another great innovator and brought her on the team. She began setting up a fundraising effort, including a calendar photo shoot, events, etc. We sat down monthly with the group who had "owned" the project for years to get them involved and keep them up to speed; and to see how we could move this forward together. We expected them to be excited about fundraising and moving it forward, but they weren't. The reaction was to own the project and prevent us from doing anything more. They let us know they had reached out to the parks department to get a letter that they were the "official" organization that would make decisions for the project. In over a dozen years, this group had raised virtually none of the estimated $350,000 needed. What they were doing wasn't working. The public had no *awareness* about the spring. This group lacked vision, but they wanted control. They didn't want to do the demanding work to *restore* the spring; they wanted to talk about it.

It was increasingly clear this group had no interest in moving the restoration forward, and ultimately, we walked away. We certainly could have expended a great deal of effort in fighting *GOWG Syndrome*, and I'm confident we could do the project without support from that group, but it would have been a life-zapping enterprise, and there were bigger fish to fry in my life. Beware of *GOWG Syndrome*, and don't let people afflicted with it derail your efforts, if you can avoid it.

Haters Gonna Hate

The truth is, sometimes there are haters. And haters gonna hate. I guess we can call this the Taylor Swift law. You can't spend your time, your energy, or your life worrying about the haters. Just innovate better and bigger and live larger, and you will make the only statement that matters. If you're a hater, hate away. I'm gonna just keep on doing me, and I would encourage you to learn to do the same.

For many people I talk to, the key is to learn how to care about other people's opinion less. If you didn't care, it wouldn't be so difficult to proceed through resistance. And in my experience, haters are people who secretly want to be you. Let them pine away, but for the love of all that is holy, don't give the haters any more of your time.

Parting Thoughts...

Building your armor is about toughening up your mental resilience for when you encounter resistance to your innovation efforts. It *will* happen and learning how to deal with tricky situations is an important part of the equation for those of us who are serial civic innovators. The public arena will rough you up if you're unprepared to endure criticism, and if we're going to keep fighting systems that need to change, because it is so important, we need to know that we can stay strong and encourage others to do the same. So consider the source, ignore the *GOWGs* and just keep going!

SELL IT

The truth is, we are in a fight for resources. For people's time. For people's money. For their attention. If we aren't good at selling our ideas, then we'd better start getting good. At the end of the day, our ability to influence an audience and connect others with a message will allow us to succeed or fail. That's just the truth. So, we need to learn how to tell a story. We must develop skills that help us deliver a message to an audience. We need to become story tellers.

Did you know that nobody wanted to work with Alexander Fleming, the man who discovered penicillin? He was generally unlikable and was unable to clearly articulate the value and possibility of his discovery. It was those who came after him that realized its potential and told, and sold, the story. Without this salesmanship, penicillin might not have saved millions of lives.

Share Stories

The most effective way to sell a concept is to sell its story. Practice telling your story. Find the great narrative that tells a compelling tale. There are several techniques you can use to create a remarkable story, but remarkable stories typically have some of the same key features, so these might help you get started:

- *Protagonist*—who or what is our hero? What idea will save the day? Who supports it?
- *Obstacles*—what has been hard about getting to this stage of the idea? What are the things still to overcome? How will you accomplish them?
- *Plot twist*—what event seemed like a road block, but was a problem solved? What was the paradigm shift that occurred?
- *Context*—what were the circumstances surrounding the idea? What was the starting paradigm?
- *Ask*—most exceptional stories ask us to believe in something or look at things in a new light. What is it you want from your listener? How can you be most effective at asking for it?

You may not need these elements in every story, but these concepts are important parts of great stories. And storytelling, emotional but rooted in fact, can be one of the most effective ways to get support for your ideas.

We should consider how we connect the audience with the human-level impact or how much time or money it could save. We can describe how it solves a problem in a unique way and makes someone's life just a little bit better. Weaving a narrative for important presentations, or summarizing the idea in an elevator pitch, are critical elements of getting innovation buy-in and support. So we should know our story and then share it.

Walk The Line: Passion Not Zealousness

When selling a story, passion is an essential element to inspiring others. When people see others with passion, they can become excited themselves. Passion is infectious and can help people get behind your great idea with energy and enthusiasm.

Zealousness is different. Zealousness is passion gone awry. Passion gets people excited. Zealousness turns them off. And it is a line to be aware of, because passion is critical to getting people on board. That's why I encourage everyone to develop an "I believe" statement and to help others play to their passions, but passion and zeal are not the same.

Zealousness is insistent and aggressive. Passion is inviting and exciting. Be sure you don't go too far off the mark but be sure to be excited about your idea. Passion will help move a person who is at a zero to a five. Zealousness is about your needs, not theirs. Remember that when telling the story of your idea. Is it coming from a place of passion or zeal?

Know Your Paradigm

Not every environment for innovation is created equal. Some environments are ready for innovation and some are not. Understanding the organization's readiness for innovation depends on the culture, change fatigue, and the support and commitment of higher-level management. To understand organizational readiness, or our paradigm, we need to evaluate innovation readiness in the organization. This includes understanding the practice of innovation, the intention of the organization and the structure of your organization's innovation efforts. We need to perform an assessment on our organizational readiness for innovation.

This is also an important part of "selling" our story better. Without understanding how ready our organization is, we might bypass someone critical or spend time on a project that ultimately won't be supported. There are always ways to sell an idea, but we can be far more effective at selling if we know what kind of support we are dealing with in the organization and where there are pockets of resistance.

Consider whether your community is conservative or liberal—what the politics are and who has the power. Consider whether it is the mayor or commissioners, or whether the administration has more influence. Focus on making powerful friends, not powerful enemies. Think about what directors are influencers and who else might help impact the ideas success. Consider your organization's ability to handle change. As you think about all these concepts, you will begin to understand more about how to convince an audience that your innovative concept is worth supporting—and where you might encounter resistance or a need to educate.

Sound-Bite Thinking

Celebrated quotes are sound bites. Marketing slogans are sound bites. Stump speeches by politicians are sound bites. Sound bites are everywhere. Because they work.

The truth is, people remember and repeat sound bites. Regrettably, too many people think in them as well. Iconic phrases like "Just Do It" and "I'm Loving It" are classic and are immediately associable with brands that we know—for good or bad. Our culture encourages this from sensational headlines to jingles on TV and politicians delivering highly polished stump speeches.

The reason that politicians deliver stump speeches is because they work. In a world where many people don't care to understand the nuances of an issue, the world encourages sound bite thinking. This thinking discourages discussion and discourse, leading to more entrenched beliefs about what is right.

While sound bites are not useful for us to understand an issue in any meaningful way, people repeat sound bites because they can attach memorable words to the emotions and call for action on an issue. When people are attached to sound bites, and they repeat them, they spread the idea and the belief. This is useful for increasing awareness and buy-in as the project goes on. Therefore, it is important to know the ONE THING you want someone to take away from your idea or your pitch. You need to know your sound bite because we want people to spread the message of our innovation to more people, so we should make it easy. Less than 10 words—simple. What sound bite captures the essence of your idea?

Know Your Elevator Pitch

This is your expanded sound bite. If you were riding an elevator with someone for 30 seconds, how would you convince them this is a promising idea? What is your "elevator pitch"? Developing a pitch that takes 30 seconds will distill your message down to its purest form.

An elevator pitch is a brief, persuasive speech that you use to spark interest in what your organization does. You can also use it to create interest in a project, idea, or product—or in yourself. A good elevator pitch should last no longer than a short elevator ride of 20 to 30 seconds, hence the name.

It should be interesting, memorable, and succinct. It also needs to explain what makes you—or your organization, product, or idea—unique.[xii]

Try to cut out anything that isn't relevant. Here's how your pitch could come together:

"My team develops electronic citizen interaction points that are simple and easy-to-use. This means that citizens can spend time on other important tasks. Unlike other communities, we built an application that allows our citizens to get the information they need in the way they need it the first time. This means that, on average, 92 percent of our citizens who interact with us are happy with their first interaction and use us again. So, how does your community handle citizen engagement?"

As you can see, this statement is clear, it differentiates us from others, and it is less than 30 seconds.

Build Your Red Team

Build your *red team*. I named it a "red team" because their job is to bloody me up on any presentation so that the elected officials or public don't get to. We do this for each other. This team agrees to view each other's presentations and be completely candid and honest *before* it is presented at a higher level. Consider it a *Blame-Free Autopsy* of your presentation. Your *red team* will help keep an eye on whether the presentation is effective, whether the visuals work, whether your presentation was attention-getting, and whether there are lingering questions or unneeded information. The team agrees to provide these services to each other and to help build support for making great presentations.

Be Bright. Be Brief. Be Gone.

Yes, it's a brilliant adage for effective communication and about as easy as it gets. Be bright, because if you're not excited about what you're saying, why would the audience be? Be brief, because everyone's time is valuable, and too often we forget to focus on our audience's needs, not our own. And be gone; when you get the answer, or input you are looking for, leave. These are the keys to having a commanding and engaging presence in any room and will help you get a reputation for effective communication.

---

xii https://www.mindtools.com/pages/article/elevator-pitch.htm

Be Bright.

This is all about getting your energy up and engaging the room. If you're not excited about what you're talking about, why on earth would anyone else be? Here are a few guidelines to help you shine in the room. With a little practice, you'll have people hanging on your every word—or at least not checking their phones when you talk. Baby steps.

• Make eye contact. Seven to ten seconds max. When you look away, don't look down.
• Shake hands firmly.
• Stand tall. Don't slouch.
• Uncross your arms and legs.
• Smile. Genuinely.
• Break the ice to put people at ease.
• Project your voice into the room when you speak.
• Be positive in how you communicate. "Yes" gets a lot more attention than "No."
• Engage the audience where they live.
• Speak with confidence.

Be Brief.

The most effective communication is brief. Choosing what to leave out can be difficult, but it more effectively engages your audience. Most of the time in communication, less is more.

THE MOST EFFECTIVE POSTS, BLOGS, TWEETS AND TALKS ARE SHORT:
• Facebook makes you "Continue Reading" at 350 characters, which people rarely do if you haven't captured their attention.
• The most popular blogs are between 500-1200 words.
• Twitter is 280 Characters, but tweets are best between 70-100 (based on most retweets).
• TED Talks are 18 minutes max. Ignite, Disrupt and Pecha Kucha-inspired events (five- minute presentations) are gaining popularity nationwide.

When communicating, define the reason for the communication (issue, goal, etc.). Give the relevant facts—good and bad. If it's a thirty-minute presentation, make it twenty minutes. Leave out extra details that are not relevant to the "bigger picture." Try to avoid telling them everything you *want* them to know, and focus on what they *need* to know. But be prepared to answer more in-depth questions if asked. Ask only for the input or direction you need to move forward. Be timely and relevant with your information. And remember to be positive in how you communicate.

Be Gone.

And once you get the direction you need or the answer you want (i.e., once you've made the sale), *stop selling*. People mess this up all the time. Pack up, thank the audience, and move on. Don't pontificate out loud for the sake of hearing yourself speak or engage in unnecessary banter after you get the answer you need. This goes wrong as often as not, and more than a few times, I have seen a positive presentation to a council go dark *after* they got the answer they wanted simply because of continuing to engage instead of walking away. If need be, clarify that an agreement has been reached and what it is. But *move on*. Being gone is about respecting people's time. And with that said: section done.

Find The Hook

I always try to find the unique angle on any given project to create unique talking points, and as Blues Traveler said: "The hook brings you back." Try to identify if it is possible to make your idea free, or beautiful, or a first-of-its-kind, or *something*, that makes it worth paying attention to! When we were doing alley improvements using parking funds, the safety improvements we were making were unremarkable but essential, and they did not create a draw. However, the funds were limited in their use so we had to abide by the legal requirements of the fund use. But we leveraged the funds as a match. By partnering with others to add artistic elements and decorative lighting, we could take alleyway improvements adjacent to a parking garage, and turn them into an opportunity for the community to come together. This provided a hook that got the media reporting on it. Positive press allowed us to get even more people involved, including many local artists. One good story led to another good story.

When doing a government-building lobby redesign, we added a space for employee artists to be featured and held monthly "First Friday" art shows to highlight the artists, bringing positive attention from the media and creating positive interaction points with the community.

When working on the "Greenfiti" program, we partnered with a local company to buy used, recycled paint that more closely matched homeowners fence colors, slashed costs by more than 50 percent, and allowed us to source our paint from a creative business in our community, while increasing our environmental stewardship. There were multiple "hooks" in this story that allowed us to get multiple press cycles worth of attention because the media could cover different angles. These positive mentions in the media create the positive attention so often lacking in government, so see what you can do to find your hook!

Make A Splash

In an age where everything is flashy and catchy and the average resident has the attention span of a goldfish,[xiii] you had better make an impact. At times, we must deliver infotainment to get noticed. Whether it is with a compelling story or with our willingness to do something wild to get noticed, we had better make sure we have a story that is powerful, emotional, intelligent, and compelling, because that is how we get the funding and the support we need. Making a splash and drawing attention to your idea is a terrific way to get your idea to go viral and your story to get shared for free. In 2011, the award-winning Troy Library faced budget shortfalls from local taxes that continued to ratchet down their spending authority. They asked for a tax increase, but a tea party group got organized and vocal and started peppering the town with vote "no" signs all over town. Not to be deterred, an enterprising group of local activists flipped the script and started adding signs around town that said "Vote to close Troy Library August 2nd. Book burning party August 5th." This outraged the community who found book burning to be a despicable concept. People started campaigning to save the library and foil the book burners and the effort gained local, then national, then *international* media attention. Then the team behind the idea revealed their true purpose: a vote to close the library is like a vote to burn books. Ultimately, the "yes" voters turned out at a rate 382 percent higher than expected, the tax increase passed, and the library was saved—and continues to win awards for excellence. It was showmanship and infotainment at its finest. Consider your story and how you can make a splash.

Social Media Impact

And while people dedicate entire books to just this topic, it is important for us to cultivate a social media presence, promote each other's material, and support each other publicly. Just a few people can help to reshape a conversation about our innovation efforts. This includes engaging our public with contests, retweeting material about great government in action, joining groups and getting involved online. It is not enough to do remarkable things, we should make others aware of what we are doing! When determining how we could best engage the public with our fledgling sustainability program over earth month, we decided to get incentives and prizes for people to upload photos of themselves doing simple, sustainable activities. We had over 1,000 photo entries in our first year and thousands more in future years. The more people saw their friends engage, the more they wanted to engage themselves. Social media is an important part of controlling our message of innovation, educating people and spreading great ideas. If you're not already out there, consider how you might begin to build a presence to build professional support for your innovation efforts.

---

xiii http://time.com/3858309/attention-spans-goldfish/

Parting Thoughts...

It is not enough to have a great idea anymore; we must learn how to sell it. In an age of limited attention spans and limited resources, we must get noticed, and when we do, we must tell a story that makes people sit up and take notice, or stand up and get involved. We should connect our audience with facts and emotion and allow them to be a part of the experience without wasting their time. We must sell innovation to be successful, so let's get serious about being amazing storytellers.

LESSONS FROM LOSING

While teasing out the key lessons for how to create *Sustainovation*, I also considered some of my less-than-stellar pilot projects and what happened. In keeping with the spirit of being honest and conducting *Blame-Free Autopsies*, my own included, I have messed up many times and been run through the ringer on "failed" projects, both publicly and privately. I have no problem talking about it, and I hope you can learn from it, so in that spirit, here's what I learned from doing it the *wrong* way. These are my lessons from losing—from failing—and I'm going to keep it real. In my experience, any one of these can derail you, but most of them we can prevent or head-off by being thoughtful and strategic about the situation. These are just the ones that seem to be common themes in my career for unsuccessful programs or pilots.

Fear Of Change

First, and this is not a shocker, but it is certainly at the top of the list. This is about knowing your paradigm and knowing that sometimes you must do a lot of work on the front end to get some people comfortable with change. And sometimes you can't get key people on board. When strategy and culture collide, culture wins, so in many cases, we need to do more front-work to avoid this. Two great tools to help mitigate this fear are using small scale pilot projects to warm people up and bringing people in during the brainstorming phase. This will generally become less of an issue as *Sustainovation* begins to permeate the organization. I find it helpful to clearly state the intended goal and to be very specific about perceived obstacles so that any, and all, objections are clearly identified. This is helpful, as it provides a chance for the fearful to vent concerns and for the innovator to obtain a list of specific concerns to begin to solve around. Fear of change is a powerful motivator, so beware of how you address people's comfort with this.

Location

Just like in real estate, the three most important things in any pilot project are location, location, location. Do whatever you can when initially piloting your ideas to find the most visible and viable location, at least for the first pilot. There is sometimes a tendency to do an "equity" push during selecting pilot locations, but we need to avoid any locations that might create additional barriers for our project. Whenever possible, we need to select locations with the highest visibility for our pilot project. I have several examples in my career where the incorrect location submarined the project. The reverse is also true: An excellent location can generate interest and results that allow us to iterate better. Location matters, so select the right location.

Awareness

Like the right location, we need effective marketing around our projects to raise awareness. A visible location, an eye-catching logo, a great *Sniglet*, a highly visible promo, a successful social media campaign, ad space in the paper or radio or guerilla marketing—whatever it takes to raise awareness and go viral on your project! Be warned: This is not *always* the case, as sometimes it is necessary to keep awareness low on certain pilots that might be more politically dangerous, so be mindful of whether you want to raise awareness or to work under the radar to provide your concept. But if you want to raise awareness, be sure to be aggressive about raising visibility.

Chronic GOWG Syndrome

As I previously identified, this is *Grumpy Old White Guy* (GOWG) *Syndrome*. When describing this earlier, I noted that this is not limited to old white guys, nor are all old white guys subject to this condition, but I use this phrase to talk about a personality style that is the enemy of innovation. Chronic *GOWG Syndrome* is characterized by limited vision and a need for control; however, it can affect any gender, race, nationality, team, etc. If you've encountered this, it embodies the principles of "the way we've always done it." When unified with other people affected by *GOWG Syndrome*, they can create a wall of resistance that can be a challenge to break down in any organization. While the Tahama Springs project I referenced earlier highlighted a fitting example of how this can create a problem for the innovator, *GOWG Syndrome* has influenced three of my more visible early-career losses, so be mindful of this syndrome as you innovate.

Market Research vs Personal Passion

This is another divergence in the innovation game. Sometimes the market research simply isn't there to support it. It just isn't. There isn't enough demand to support the idea becoming permanent. Sometimes there is. This is where our zeal or personal passion (or the personal passions of others) can cloud our judgment, and without proper market research, we will find ourselves pushing an idea with no traction uphill.

At Adams County, we launched a program idea from our innovation academy team that seemed like it was wildly successful—and wasn't. The need: Adams County has one of the highest Hispanic populations in the state, many of whom speak only Spanish. Not exactly a new challenge, but because of policy restrictions at the time, our employees were not allowed be reimbursed for language classes at a college or university unless it was in pursuit of a degree. The team explored a variety of options and came to an idea we called "TryLingual." The pilot program was a multilingualism effort using Rosetta Stone and a series of small, temporary, revised incentives to encourage our employees to become a conduit to our Spanish-speaking community. We conducted a study of employees who indicated an interest in the program's concept and determined what was the most favored method for learning (in class, lunch hour, Rosetta Stone, etc.), and Rosetta Stone was the narrow winner.

When we opened the program for sign-up, we sold it out in under two minutes! Participants agreed to reach designated learning milestones every quarter to continue participation in the program. The overwhelming enthusiasm for the pilot seemed to indicate an immense success.

The truth is, people like the idea of winning a contest. But signing up isn't showing up. They liked the *idea* of learning a language, but they didn't like learning it nearly as much. It's arduous work and hard to fit in with all of life's other priorities. The number of participants who had used the system at the one-month check-in was less than 25 percent! So, we sent out reminders, nudging participants to hit their achievement marks by the first quarter check-in so they wouldn't risk forfeiting the license to another interested party. The wait list was long, after all.

But at the first quarter mark, only 12 percent of participants had reached the goal. It became clear that reassigning all those licenses, which was an incredibly manual process, but allowed, would be a nightmare. The team met and discussed what to do, and it was decided to let it play out without the penalties, see what the result would be, and learn lessons. In the end, only six people completed the process in the agreed-upon timeframe.

While we had conducted market research, we failed to ask the right questions, and about intent to follow through, and while Rosetta Stone was the preferred method to learn, it wasn't the *right* method to learn. People found it difficult to carve out time. The platform was confusing. The goals were too aggressive. Learning a language is demanding work, and people's passion and enthusiasm waned.

But just like the law of unintended consequences always shows, some unexpected things happened. The high-profile nature of the pilot caused the organization to examine its policies related to reimbursement for college courses, and it now reimburses language classes, as well as certificate programs, a meaningful change in policy that would not have come about without the pilot. Hence, the pilot did address and innovate one aspect of the intended goal, a change in policy, but failed to directly train the organization to handle the growing multilingual need in the community. Which brings me to...

Law of Unintended Consequences

The law of unintended consequences. We cannot predict all the results of a pilot; otherwise we wouldn't have to run them. When we tried a new type of biodiesel, we didn't test the new blend for proper cold hardiness testing because it was expensive according to our contract, and the biodiesel fuel gelled up, setting back our efforts. We rewrote the contract so that free monthly fuel testing would be required and were able to catch a future (non-biodiesel) related fuel issue because we changed the disincentives that were in place. When incentives create undesirable effects, the law of unintended consequence might be in play.

For example, in the 1980s, there was a major push to eliminate chlorofluorocarbons (CFCs) from aerosol sprays because the CFCs were eating holes in the ozone layer. The hole in the ozone layer was allowing damaging ultraviolet radiation through our atmosphere, creating dangerous environmental consequences. Hence the ban on CFCs in 1989. Fast forward 25 years, and the ban on CFCs is allowing the ozone hole to stitch back up—but it is also increasing the rate of localized climate change over the South Pole. Essentially, it is causing one problem while fixing another because the ozone is trapping gases locally. This is the law of unintended consequence. This is the unknown. The unforeseen.

Sometimes it's force majeure. This is Latin for "shit happens." It's just the act of God that ends your project. Beyond your control. The weather doesn't cooperate. The pipes burst. The internet goes down. Life.

The law of unintended consequence and force majeure have submarined otherwise great ideas more than once in my career. While you cannot plan for this, preparation and resiliency can minimize its effects on your success. There will always be elements beyond our thought or control, and the unknown is just that—unknown. So be prepared, make your own luck and just know that acts of God happen. Force majeure happens. Shit...well shit happens too. Don't be surprised; be ready.

No Data To Back It Up

I have seen countless pilots fail because there is no data to back them up. This is a pitfall I learned to avoid early on in my career, because my undergraduate degree centered largely on being good at math and using data to drive decision-making. My greatest successes came in using numbers, and I'm good at math, so for me, using data was always part of my projects. But in watching many other people launch pilots, I have seen more people with great ideas fail to measure their project's results and ultimately pay the price when it comes time to justify the project and its impact. Without the numbers, it is hard to get the support we need. And when I have failed to heed this advice myself, it has almost always backfired.

I know it is hard to make an argument that "facts matter" with politics in America in the state they are in, but the plain truth is that bridges, infrastructure, parks, and emergency services are all subject to fact, not feeling. People care about how quickly the police and fire departments arrive when they need them, or that the bridges or levees don't collapse. The facts matter. Science matters. And data is the key to driving the right outcomes.

But you also need to recognize that data collection can be tedious at times, so minimizing the impact of data collection is important to getting regular and accurate data from our team. If it is a huge burden, people won't want to measure, so we need to make sure we only measure those things that *move the needle*. Data must be accurate as well, so we should find the most automated, reliable, and consistent way we can to measure it, because inaccurate information is the same as no data at all (and may even be worse).

"No Money"

So many times, I hear this as the reason people cannot get things done. "We have no money."

Many pilots don't get off the ground for this reason. One thing I find so often is that people don't take the time to fully understand how their organization's budget works. They don't take the time to understand how money is transferred and budgeted for and what the rules are for getting it and holding onto it. Here are a few key questions you can answer to help understand how well you understand the funding options in your organization—and how you might find funding:

- Can you strike a deal with the budget department to take savings—even a portion—from one project and apply it to another?
- Can you roll money over from year to year or take money from another account to fund your idea?
- How can you get your idea considered as part of the annual budget process?
- How do revenues work, and can revenues help to offset the costs?

- If you need seed money, can you forge a public-private partnership to make it happen?
- If you need major funding, are there grants available?
- Are there any one-off, but dedicated, funding streams you might be able to tap to get the project off the ground or to leverage other dollars?
- Are there federal funds or non-profit partners?
- Can you put together a fundraising and awareness event?
- How about GoFundMe or crowdsourcing?

Taking the time to sit down and think through all the possible funding options with the budget staff at your organization is a critical part of understanding how to get money and how to hold money. Buy them coffee and have the budget team show you the entire process so you can be more effective at getting the money you need to get your idea off the ground. But if you're still having problems with getting the funds you need once you understand how the money moves, think about how compelling your case is (or isn't) and if you can better communicate its urgency. In today's world, it is more often and more common for persistence to be the issue rather than actual funding. If you are dedicated to your idea, and you believe it is the right thing to do, be patient and don't let "no money" be the thing to stop you. Find a creative way to get the funding you need to prove a concept or build your case, and then look for more money with a more compelling case.

Oh, and one of the other results of being able to creatively fund our projects is that people will look at us like some sort of wizard. It is rare that people explore options outside of the immediate potential solution, which is one reason this is so often a source of pilots failing. Therefore, it is met with great surprise when we are successful in getting money after someone said "no" or others could not figure out how to get it done. Finding funding will also help establish with others our dedication and commitment to ideas we believe in, a powerful message about our leadership, which can help when building momentum on future projects. We started a city-wide recycling program with $229. We funded a community garden using revenue from recycled ink cartridges. We made major improvements in the downtown by leveraging dedicated parking funds. And on and on. So often I hear money be the reason someone won't even try a pilot project, when really it is often an excuse. Don't let money stop you.

Politics Trumps Performance

At the end of the day, sometimes politics trumps performance. Sometimes...

- you will be unable to shake off the politics of a situation
- all the facts in the world will not convince people
- people will choose to make the illogical choice, no matter what you do
- people will fear change more than they hope for success

- politics and unfair perception will beat out a great idea or great innovation

It can be exceedingly difficult in these moments to not become bitter or jaded by the experience, but just know that it is okay if you face this kind of defeat. It means that you are moving the needle and that people need to exert their power—a common *GOWG Syndrome* symptom. Life goes on. You are plunging off into the wilderness and making maps. And this will provoke political responses at times. Sometimes it is literal politics from politicians, and sometimes it is internal organizational politics or community dynamics. If you're doing things that matter and shaking the paradigm of your community up, you will face these kinds of stinging defeats. I have repeatedly run afoul of politicians, as well as politically-minded ladder climbers, during my career, and I have faced hard defeats for political reasons at times, but I am resilient, I am good at what I do, and I am not afraid to get fired. This gives me the freedom to keep it real when others would balk at saying the truth. If you can, be known for not wasting people's time, for being direct, and for being fearless. I encourage you to be fact-based, to make intelligent decisions backed by data, and to accept that you will be beaten by politics from time to time. Have a moment to be pissed off, shake it off, and move on. People expect us to react to defeat the same way they would, which makes it even more surprising when we don't. Don't show the politicians that it sucked. Just move right on. Act like you've been there before, and you will find yourself there less often.

I remember a project where we had figured out how to leverage parking dollars to increase the safety of an adjacent park by using LED lighting. The park was surrounded by paid parking, which meant the park could receive some improvements that would "increase the safety of people using parking meters," and since people used this park as a cut through, making it better lit would serve several important purposes. This pilot also proved the value of LED light technology to the local utility, which had only been minimally supportive of LED light adoption at that point. It had all the elements of a win-win, but at the time, the leadership was very risk-averse and hyperpolitical, meaning they only liked to be associated with "winning" projects and partisan politics ruled the dialogue. If one person was "for" something, another person was "against" it. Politics mattered more than performance. A project that took over a year and had the potential to be a win-win, turned into an embattled discussion about politics, not performance. This has happened several times in my career, and these are some of the hardest moments, but now that I know it will happen, I'm prepared for it.

Politics will trump performance. Know it, and when it happens, shake it off, keep doing you, learn from it if you can, and move on. That will show the next person that politics may win, but that they should do the right thing anyway. That's how you build a culture of innovation. You prove that it matters, and you keep doing it, regardless.

My Ego

My ego has ended a few great projects. Yes, my hubris has been to blame for bringing down a few of my favorite projects. It's a hard thing to admit to myself, but the truth is, it can be a hard balance to strike at times. Innovation requires a lot of competing forces to align and, by its very nature, makes many people uncomfortable. While building personal and emotional armor can be important to shouldering criticism, there are times where I missed the human element. There have been times where I overestimated my own cunning and made a strategic miscalculation, or proceeded without the support I needed. It's an occupational hazard and I learned from each one. Having confidence in your abilities is crucial, but that can also leave you with blind spots. Try to recognize those moments when your passion has turned to zeal, or when the cost of resistance is too high. Pick your battles and try to keep your ego out of it as much as possible. And when you do have less-than-stellar moments, which we all have, own it and learn from them.

Parting Thoughts...

I hope these lessons from losing and the candid delivery will help you avoid similar pitfalls. Undoubtedly each person will face their own battles and challenges as they learn their best path to innovation, but these are elements that have derailed me. Some are avoidable; some aren't. But beware these *Lessons from Losing*!

SUSTAINOVATION

We have explored why innovation is difficult, how we can unlock our creativity, how we can grow our ideas, how to construct a good pilot, what it takes to build a team, how we take action, how we grow thicker skin, how we sell our ideas to others, and how to avoid common pitfalls. The lessons up to this point have been all about growing our personal ability to implement sustainable innovation, but what about things we can do to embed and structure innovation into our organizations?

Usually organizational leaders ask me two questions: "What can I do to build a culture of innovation and make it sustainable?" and "where do we begin?"

This section covers some techniques we can use to begin building a culture of *Sustainovation* in our organization and where we should look to start.

In my experience, building *Sustainovation* is about time, persistence and setting up the circumstances to succeed. There are five key elements that contribute to a successful innovation environment that need to be an intentional discussion. You do not need all of these in place to succeed, but you do need to have a conversation as an organization or leadership team about each. First is an Innovation Fund. As we know, that which gets funded, gets prioritized. An Innovation Academy helps us to do deep-dive training and cultivate an environment of intentional innovation collaboration and immersive learning. Be intentional about discussing and measuring *Innovation Value*. Invest in your employees Education. Grow their skills, invest in their abilities, mentor them and turn them loose to help train others. This is how a culture is built. Employees teaching employees. And last, Structure. How will innovation function in your organization? Who will be responsible for aggregating ideas and information? Set up your Structure to succeed.

These techniques are my *Sustainovation* FAVES. Although I will unravel this acronym in this chapter, the words spell the acronym FAVES, making it easy to remember:

- Fund
- Academy
- Value

- Education
- Structure

As an organization, I believe if we address the FAVES, we will begin to set up our organization for *sustained* innovation success. Let's examine the FAVES a little closer and then take a look at where we can begin.

Fund

One tool available to every organization is an innovation fund. It takes very little to get started and is a fantastic way to create some room for innovation. There are many variables that go into executing a successful innovation fund and many possible ways to do it, but here are some basic guidelines I have used successfully in the past and will help along your way:

- Determine the goal of your innovation fund. What does success look like? What is the success rate we want? Too much success means not enough risk.
- Determine fund size, scope and conditions.
- What's the right size? Large or small? Too large, and there is no urgency and greater likelihood to be abused; too small, and it says, "we aren't serious about innovation," so think carefully about this decision.
- One-time or year-over-year expenses? I have always used one-time funding, as it keeps it less likely to be abused with FTE requests and is significantly easier to handle administratively, but it's your call.
- How many times per year are you going to have the application process open? I recommend limiting it to twice per year to create scarcity and a more manageable process, but again, that is up to you.
- Micro-grants only? Or can someone apply for the whole fund? Are there fund application limits?
- Sell the concept (if necessary). This is a lot easier if you're the boss.
  » What is your compelling why?
  » Prepare the elevator pitch and executive summary docs.
  » "This fund is the equivalent of the most creative, most effective employee you have." The fact is, if the employees don't come up with amazing ideas, the organization doesn't spend the funds.
  » Pitch the concept to leadership. Prepare to wait one year as it goes through "the budget cycle" if need be.
- Get a senior sponsor who believes in it with you. Their role is to help sell it to the organization and shepherd it in budget and leadership discussions.
- Install clear and reasonable controls—fiscal oversight, accountability, goals, metrics, etc. Do not make these onerous or overly rigorous, nor should this be ignored. Controls are important, not bureaucracy.

- Determine the selection process and make it clear to employees. People should know how they are being evaluated before applying.
- Pilots *only*. This is not to fund FTEs, your failed IT project or your unfulfilled budget request. It is to fund pilot projects that are limited in scope and scale and have a clear goal. Trust me, make this part clear.
- Develop the application process.
  - » I recommend an easy one or two-page form.
  - » Determine 4-6 key questions—short and to the point.
  - » What is the right scale? Scale of 1-10? Score out of 100?
  - » Innovation Fund applications open for one month or shorter, if possible.
- Applicants submit innovation fund form.
  - » Paper or online? Other methods—video, etc?
- Develop selection committee structure.
  - » 6-10 people.
  - » Cross-functional and cross-departmental if possible.
  - » Be thoughtful about selection committee design: We need overlap to continue continuity but one-half of the team can rotate out annually. This committee should turn over at least every three years as the goal is to involve people.
  - » Selection committee reviews and provides feedback, comments, concerns before interview.
- Applicants are required to have 15 to 30-minute interviews with selection committee to fully explain, vet idea, and help develop it further.
  - » If needed, ideas are revised and resubmitted.
- Selection team develops scores based on criteria and determines ranking and funding level recommendations.
  - » What happens when someone doesn't get funds? How are they notified?
  - » Can they apply again?
- Executive leadership is presented with funding recommendations and makes final determination of the awards. It is critical that they understand that the role of this executive team is to be mindful of any political concerns, raise awareness and serious concerns, and ensure support from the top leadership.
- Funds are awarded. Celebrate with the recipients, and market the awards to the employees so they are aware the funds are available and that people are using them.
- Monthly or quarterly check-ins with fund recipients to monitor progress and provide support as needed
- Market projects as appropriate to raise awareness and encourage recognition (remember: idea generation and implementation credit!).
- Conduct updates as needed, and when completed, conduct a *Blame-Free Autopsy* with project managers and any available team members to talk about what worked

and what didn't. Memorialize lessons while they are still "fresh" in the innovation project manager's mind.

- Provide at least an annual update to your organization's executive team and elected leadership on the fund, its projects, its successes, and its "failures." When possible and appropriate, have employees be presenters to sharpen skills and show impact. Be sure to be bright, be brief, and be gone!
- Use updates and project stories to sell the fund both internally and externally and to build momentum.
- Lather. Rinse. Repeat.

In my experience, selling an innovation fund is about helping people understand what it is, what it is not, how it will be used, and how it will be regulated. It is not an IT fund, a way around the budget process for major initiatives, nor is it used to fund full-time employees or whole-scale organizational changes. It is used for one-time pilot projects that are limited in scope and scale.

By using an innovation fund, we can mitigate the organization's risk, and by empowering our innovation academy members to be responsible for the organization's innovation, we are creating a pipeline of innovation and risk reduction that permeates the organization's culture. The last fund I was a part of funded 22 of 26 applications. Not everything gets funded and that's okay—we are taking shared risks. By defraying risk among multiple pilot projects, we insulate ourselves from individual failure risk.

In my experience, a well-built innovation fund and well-trained innovation academy can raise employee morale and help launch a pipeline of creativity for your organization. It provides a means for employees to feel heard and engages them in a way that can transform your organization. Yes, an innovation fund is a great equalizer in building *Sustainovation*. Now how about that academy?

Academy

In my opinion, one of the best ways to develop great innovation teamwork is to put together the framework for an innovation academy and begin training. Use the concepts in this book as a starting point for a discussion with your team. Have a *Sustainovation* book club project. Set up some of the challenges and work through them together. Practice your skills at being a *Map Maker* and *Map Follower*.

I have done several versions of an innovation academy, but they all have common elements:

- Train on the principles of Sustainovation. Obviously, this book is based on principles I teach my academies.
- Ice breaker/team builder for the first session—anything that sets people off their game a little.

- One to three hours every month for six to eight months.
- Create a diverse team from across the organization. I have had people who were voluntold, and those who applied to be there. Applying or sponsoring talent is the right method in my experience.
- To graduate the program, there is a team "capstone pilot project" to demonstrate capability and implementation ability.
- When appropriate, use "graduates" to oversee the innovation fund projects in the future.

These are the basics, but each organization is unique in its needs. Obviously, this book is the genesis for the materials I use in my academies, and there is a lot of value in dialogue, interaction, and practicing with people, so I encourage you to experiment with others on concepts in this book. Regardless of how we construct it, an innovation academy can be a wonderful way, with or without dedicated innovation staff, to increase the readiness of our organization for *Sustainovation*.

Value

Another great tool we can use is *Innovation Value*. Yes, you can measure the value of innovation, and you should. When we were pioneering the concepts in civic innovation, our community had a conservative leaning, so the models of social innovation pioneered in Boston, San Francisco, and Philadelphia, our peers at the time, were not going to work for us. So we sat down and started talking about how innovation has value, and how all we had to do was get better at measuring it. Since each innovation has a diminishing value over time, innovation must be constantly happening to continue to have value; otherwise that value fades over time. Innovation is a cycle and must be continuously renewed, so we developed a method to measure innovation called *Innovation Value*:

Innovation Value (IV) = reasonable Net Present Value of (Actual Cost Savings + Efficiency Value (EV))

Here's one example of how we used it: In Colorado Springs, the Streets division had a large fleet with a lot of old, outdated equipment, because the replacement budget has not been available. Sound familiar? However, when the city sells equipment, the proceeds would go back into the general fund "black hole," meaning the Streets division would have no direct incentive to sell equipment. In addition, the Budget department knew very little of the operational needs for the equipment and relied on the Streets division to tell them. Hence the fleet size grow over time. Shift the paradigm. Working with our Budget and Streets teams, we struck a deal where the Streets team would get all the proceeds from the *one-time* sale of equipment to invest in new equipment. The Streets division now had an incentive to do everything they could to trim the fleet and make thoughtful choices about what equipment best suited its 21st century needs. Changing the incentive changed the behavior.

The Streets division benefitted from new equipment. The Budget department benefitted from reduced maintenance and fuel costs. A win-win. Thus, the Streets division identified and eliminated 69 pieces of equipment, yielding $590,000 in one-time money that was reinvested in six pieces of critical equipment AND reduced the maintenance costs to the general fund by $150,000 per year. So, what is the *Innovation Value* of this?

Innovation Value is the sum of the net present value of Actual Cost Savings plus Efficiency Value. "Efficiency Value" comes from any funds that are reinvested into the organization—like the $590,000 reinvested in mission-critical equipment. Since these funds are not actually saved but are reinvested, we need to identify that separately.

In the example above, the *Innovation Value* is the reasonable NPV of the reduced maintenance plus the reinvested funds (the Efficiency Value). Since the maintenance requirement will be virtually nil for the first three years because of warranties, one can choose three years as the reasonable NPV period. I also typically use a "discount rate" of six percent, but your finance team can help you set that. It should be part of the discussion. As a result, the *Innovation Value* is:

Innovation Value= 3-year NPV of $150,000 annually (~$410,000) + $590,000 = $1,000,000

Innovation Value can be measured for most things. The goal is to translate time, attention, effectiveness, efficiency, and productivity into dollars. It's a conversion, if you will. For example, if we build a new process that reduces the amount of time it takes for residents to fill out a form by 15 minutes and eliminates the need for a paper form, we can calculate the *Innovation Value*. We can find the average value of a resident's time by using labor statistics from our local metropolitan area; we can determine an average wage and therefore an average value of residents' time in our region.[xiv] We can value employee time in a comparable way, using an average wage for our employees from human resources or payroll. We can refine these figures as needed, but we can assign value to the time. As you develop a definition, document any assumptions you make before the next innovation comes along. For example, if there were 12,000 forms filled out annually, and it is 15 minutes' savings per form, and $3,500 in reduced printing and handling costs, our *Innovation Value* is:

Innovation Value= 5-year NPV of $3,500 + 5-year NPV of (12,000 x .25 × $25 per hour) = $330,670

There are also websites and studies that can help translate things like morale, satisfaction, and beauty into quantifiable figures you can use, although I would argue that not everything should be translated into the almighty dollar. We just have to ensure that the definition is appropriate and agreed upon for your community, so use this definition as a starting point to have your own conversation about *Innovation Value*.

---

xiv https://www.bls.gov/bls/blswage.htm

By tracking every innovation project in this way, we can create a portfolio of projects that collectively shows the power of *Sustainovation* to the organization. In 2012, the portion of *Innovation Value* directly generated by our team was equal to 89 percent of our total office costs (salary, benefits, operating, etc.), and by 2013 we demonstrated we had delivered equal to more than 175 percent of the total cost of our office. In any fiscally-responsible government organization, it is critical that we find a way to define the value of innovation in a way that leadership can understand and agrees with.

What created the most value from defining *Innovation Value* was that we could have a meaningful conversation about the value of innovation and demonstrate that our office was saving the organization far more than our value on the government payroll and our office budget. By having discussions around the value of innovation in our organization, we began to recognize the business case for innovation, and it became more "normal" and less scary. It became more sustainable. It created a language around innovation and how it was valued. It also provided a clear metric anyone in the organization could use to value innovation.

There are some key questions we should consider as an organization when examining our definition of *Innovation Value*:

- Is it only direct wages and direct costs that count?
- How about benefits, such as medical or retirement?
- Do we include sunk costs? Administrative overhead?
- How about money reinvested, but not saved?
- What about other value such as engagement, morale, beauty, equity, and productivity? Do we want to measure or value that in our calculation or not?
- Will we allow only a percentage of our *Innovation Value* based on our contribution to a given project or track all of it?
- Do we want to set a standard net present value period or discount rate?
- How do we value risk/reward or unintended consequences? Remember we are trying to push our organizations!

By determining and agreeing on our definition of *Innovation Value*, the organization can define the way in which it values innovation—allowing employees to have a clear definition of how it will be valued. And as you learn more, feel free to revise the definition—just make sure the way it is valued is fully known! The most important thing is that there is an agreed upon measurement for how it will be valued to begin.

Education

I believe the continuous, *meaningful* education of our employees is another area where the innovation cultural battle is won or lost. The truth is we must rethink our employee education models. Our employees are experts in their own crafts. We have people in our organizations who know Microsoft Excel inside and out. People who know real deep-dive analytics. People who use apps. People who teach business accounting on the weekends. People who design surveys. Bi-lingual people who are patient teachers. We have yoga instructors, and fly fisherman, and master gardeners, and authors and much more among our employees. Why not train our employees to be teachers and share their experience and knowledge?

Employees are more likely to stick with an organization that values their growth and development—especially the next generation of workers. We can help our employees learn how to craft lessons, make impactful presentations and empower them to teach and train others. I have learned that the organizational pulse for innovation is heavily guided by commitment to real learning and education. Not a surprise really, but such an important organizational lever. I believe that organizational innovation can and should begin in the training and development of employees. I'm not talking about mandatory workplace trainings or vanilla leadership development or time-card classes. No, I'm talking about true investment in their growth as people. Mentoring. Coaching. Training. Guiding. Real education. From the beginning. And the ability and opportunity to share with others. Take a close look at your organization's training and development program. Ensure the training is meaningful and relevant. What opportunities exist to unlock employees?

Ask your employees what they can teach. Work on their skills to craft lessons. Look to neighboring jurisdictions and see if they have particularly excellent training classes and strike an exchange agreement. Start a mentoring program for new employees. Track consistent information about the effectiveness of the classes and trainers. Partner with a local career counselor to offer free advice to employees. Offer online training services. Invest in the education of your employees and allow them to return the favor. There are literally dozens of ways to engage in the meaningful growth and development of your employees' education. This is *Team Us* in action. Everyone contributes to the growth of the organization and this is where the growth of our organizational innovation begins to multiply as we decentralize organizational knowledge sharing.

Structure

The last of the FAVES to reckon with is your organization's innovation structure. One of the most common discussions I have with city and county managers starting an innovation program is what kind of innovation structure is "best." Best is a misleading term as the real goal is to build an innovation program so it is not dependent on one person only, but can thrive as a part of culture even with turnover. There has been a lot of debate about whether a centralized or decentralized version of organizational innovation works better. This is a false narrative. I would argue that there is no such thing as a centralized model. There is no "one oracle" of innovation, nor does any innovator worth his or her salt want that kind of pressure. My immediate goal as the head of any innovation program is to activate great innovators in the organization—it's about teaching people how to unlock their potential and helping them to clear road blocks on their way to implementation. Effective innovation is always decentralized, whether you have an innovation director or not.

With that said, I'm an enthusiastic fan of any innovation model that has a single point of accountability for actively improving the organization's innovation efforts, encouraging adoption, mitigating risk, and measuring its success. Someone who guides the organization's efforts and keeps the organization focused. We can't stumble into *Sustainovation*. We need to train it, craft it, build it, and support it, and that takes dedication. Communities can develop innovation programs without a person dedicated to leading the effort, but in my experience, innovation happens much faster and more effectively with someone who is actively engaging the organization in building its *Sustainovation*. If your organization is in that position, a person directing or managing an innovation program should ideally report to the city or county manager or the deputy manager. This person needs to have organization-wide opportunity to support innovation outside of structural bureaucracy as much as possible.

Where Do We Begin?

When starting an innovation effort, "where do we begin?" is a close follow-up to "how do we build a culture of innovation?" The truth is there is no right spot to begin, and my tongue-in-cheek, career-limiting answer would be "everywhere," but in keeping with the spirit of useful advice and useful acronyms, I recommend starting with the PEGS:

- Permission
- Elephants
- Gray
- Support

Permission

Begin where you have permission. It is important to get started on the right foot with your organized effort, so ensure that you or your team knows where they have permission to begin. Don't use the team as a weapon to "fix" another section of the organization, just define the boundaries where they have permission to begin. And that is as good a place as any to start.

Elephant

If you are a fearless *Map Maker* and want to jump right in with disruptive change, begin with taking a bite of the organization's biggest elephant. What is the smelliest, most accessible pain point for the organization? Begin there. There are usually important reasons why people avoid or fail when tackling their organizational elephants, but in my experience, it is just the determination, creativity, approach, and willingness to fail that constrains us. Try to tackle the biggest, nastiest problem you can—and rally your *Team Us* from across the organization to help eat the elephant. Learn from others who have tried to tackle it before and improve. Measure key metrics. Report out every two weeks to stay accountable. Document your efforts so you can learn from your successes and failures along the way. And there is a lot in the courage of trying to do things others fear to do, so it makes a suitable place to start for seasoned innovators looking to make an impact. Remember, this will require a large team of people to be successful, so begin to build your team and create a common vision for success. And organizational elephants have tough hides, so just know that you will encounter resistance along the way, but if you get traction, you can make an impression while returning valuable resources to the organization.

Gray

Begin with the space between. The gray areas between departments where you see opportunity, but no one "owns" the space. For example, I've had great success working on sustainability pilots, which no one in the organization "owned." I happen to have a personal passion, so it made a great fit to begin innovating. But I've also had success with existing committees, such as the awards committee or with creating annual events to address a specific

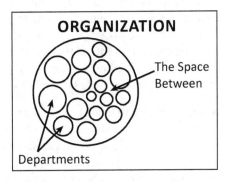

community need. There are many ways to find the space between. This approach usually gives you the chance to collaborate with a variety of diverse groups and departments, without stepping on too many toes, and potentially win important allies to your innovation cause. A word of caution: While I have found this space easiest to work in and build momentum in overall, occasionally it can get very contentious when you bump up against resistant departments or those who feel a sense of ownership, whether it is their job or not. Or even a chronic and severe case of *GOWG Syndrome*. But, starting where there is less direct organizational ownership is a wonderful place to begin.

Support

My favorite option on where to begin is to go where you are invited. This is different than permission—just because you are allowed to innovate somewhere doesn't mean you'll have support. Start where you have support. Usually an organization has at least 2-3 senior leaders who will "buy in" to trying innovative ideas. Think about areas adjacent to, but not directly in, their purview, or areas where they need the most help. If you are invited in to a department, pitch the department head on working with their team as a free resource, or ask to learn more about a problem they are facing or opportunity they want to pursue. This is a wonderful place for a *Map Follower* to start!

In my experience, PEGS are a suitable place to start for any innovation effort. Once you have demonstrated a track record of success, you may find yourself more easily able to work within departments or across organizational boundaries.

Parting Thoughts...

So, there it is: *INNOVATION IS CREATIVITY IMPLEMENTED*. By loading our proverbial "innovation kitchen" with ingredients, we are preparing ourselves to create meaningful change in our organizations. By mastering a handful of tools and techniques, we have what we need to get out and tackle bureaucracy like a boss. We know how to ask *Why?*, how to get creative and shift our perspective, how to brainstorm, and how to pilot ideas. We know how to build our *Team Us*, take action, build up our armor, and sell our ideas. We know some common pitfalls and how to hard code innovation into our organizations using *Sustainovation* FAVES.

We know where to begin and we have the power to challenge government bureaucracy with *Sustainovation*. We have the power to reinvigorate our community, and address social and economic issues in bold ways never before seen. If done properly, using and practicing the techniques in this book will help you become a stronger innovator, unlock your creativity and help create structure for your organization to build a model of *Sustainovation* that will last for years to come. My hope is that these lessons from my life as a serial innovator in government will ring true for you and stock your kitchen with the ingredients necessary to make great innovation happen!

We face tremendous challenges, but we have tremendous creativity and ability at our disposal. I hope as you unleash your unbridled creativity, and put it into action, you will share your story with me and with others and help create a world where government is synonymous, once again, with putting a man on the moon rather than with the line at the DMV. It is time for *Sustainovation* to take hold of government and disrupt it. Doing that will take dedicated innovators like you leading the charge, so welcome to the fight, and thank you for all you do for our country and your community. Now go crush it. *Team Us*.

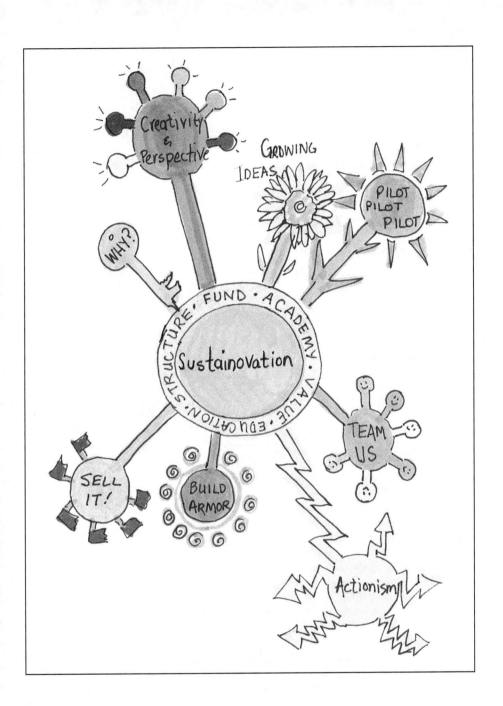

CPSIA information can be obtained
at www.ICGtesting.com
Printed in the USA
LVHW082254240619
622252LV00034B/496/P